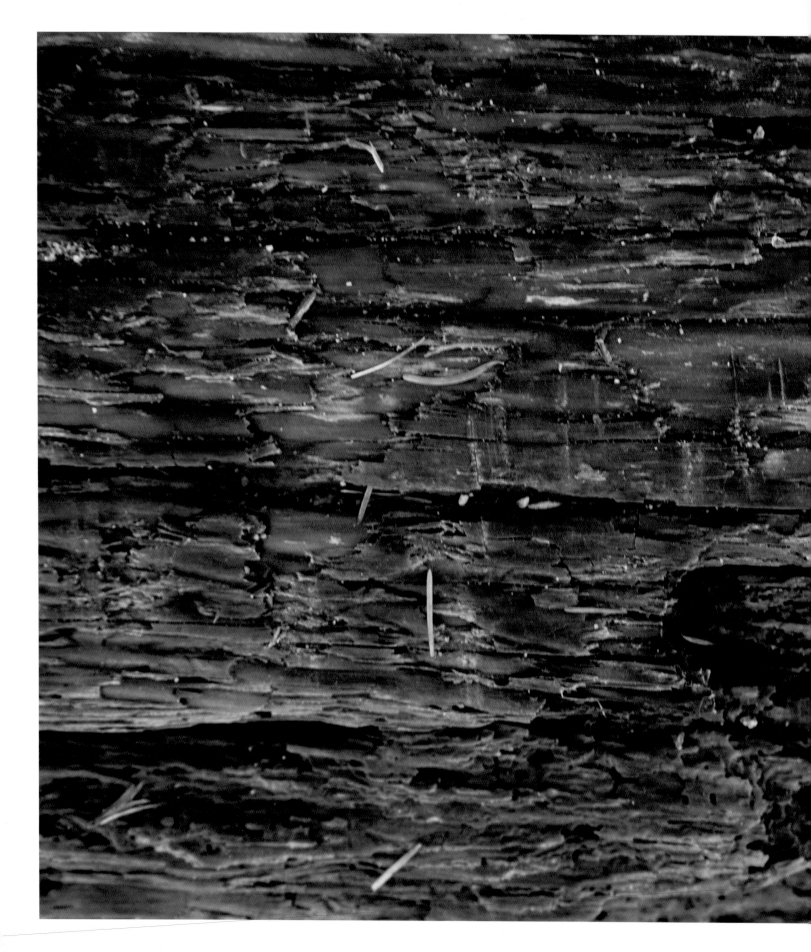

# SEA AND SMOKE

## FLAVORS FROM THE UNTAMED PACIFIC NORTHWEST

**BLAINE WETZEL**
AND **JOE RAY**

PHOTOGRAPHY BY
**CHARITY BURGGRAAF**

RUNNING PRESS
PHILADELPHIA · LONDON

Published by Running Press,
A Member of the Perseus Books Group

Books published by Running Press are available at special discounts for bulk purchases in the United States by corporations, institutions, and other organizations. For more information, please contact the Special Markets Department at the Perseus Books Group, 2300 Chestnut Street, Suite 200, Philadelphia, PA 19103, or call (800) 810-4145, ext. 5000, or e-mail special.markets@perseusbooks.com.

ISBN 978-0-7624-5378-8

Library of Congress Control Number: 2015937004

E-book ISBN 978-0-7624-5311-5

9   8   7   6   5   4   3   2
Digit on the right indicates the number of this printing

Designed by Joshua McDonnell
Edited by Kristen Green Wiewora
Typography: Brandon
Author photo on back endpaper by Steve Raichlen (www.barbecuebible.com)

Running Press Book Publishers
2300 Chestnut Street
Philadelphia, PA 19103-4371

Visit us on the web!
www.offthemenublog.com

FOR RAQUEL, OF COURSE

BLAINE


TO ELISABETH, FOR TAKING THE PLUNGE

JOE

# FOREWORD
BY GRANT ACHATZ

I stood ankle deep in steamy muck, swatted bees away from my face, skinned my knee on jagged rocks, pierced my fingers with thorns, and, with some guilt, apprehensively ended the lives of gorgeous pink trout with my bare hands, the traditional way, as it has been done on Lummi Island for more than 100 years. Not exactly what you would expect before eating one of the best meals of my life. But, without a doubt, experiences that not only shape the identity of the restaurant at Willows Inn but also help people understand the chef and his cuisine.

I knew about Blaine's work experience at Manresa and Noma after reading about him in *Food & Wine* magazine, from blogs, and from whispers coming from the James Beard house. People were talking about this magical restaurant that procured most of its ingredients from the waters, fields, woods, and forests a stone's throw from the kitchen. I heard about the commitment to simply arriving there—planes, cars, and a ferry—reminding me of the great restaurants of Europe that I put on a culinary pedestal, Bras, El Bulli, and Veyrat. This only added to my excitement and elevated my expectations. I hope this guy can cook.

I imagined the hyperfocused seriousness of a chef who was so sure of his style and convictions that it might feel preachy. He was young, twenty-six, and I feared a chef following the tsunami-size wave of popularity started in some ways as far back as Chez Pannise in this country but recently gaining enormous momentum as it evolved into what would become the New Nordic revolution for the wrong reasons.

And then the first course came.

A simple smoked mussel. That is all it was. And all of what it was. Sincere, provocative, mature, and intelligent defined the voice of Blaine Wetzel's cooking, and it immediately dispelled my previous fear. I grinned after that single mussel was gone, not because it tasted delicious, it did, but because at that moment I understood what the chef was doing. It was my "ah ha" moment, the curtain was pulled back, and I was happy. I knew then exactly why he was here on this remote, tiny island using the surrounding environment to evoke a true sense of place with his cooking. Blaine was teaching his guests about Lummi Island, telling its story through his cooking.

At one point in every chef's career, we dream of running away. Running away from the impurities that control our lives as chefs, as cooks. We dream of finding a simpler paradise removed from cars, concrete, congestion, and complications allowing us to connect to the product we cook, understanding it from seed to plant, young to mature, imperfect to optimum. Along the way, feeling the subtle nuances of the very thing we often most take for granted as cooks, the ingredients.

Blaine ran away too. But instead of apprehension and fear, he did so with determination, risk-taking confidence, and unabashed ambition directly toward the dream. And he found it.

I grew up on the edge of open wilderness, always spending as much time as possible outdoors. My family and I would hike in the Cascade Mountains and walk along the rocky beaches near our home in Olympia, Washington. I'd fish in the mountain streams, collect wild blackberries, and spend all day in the woods.

When I was fourteen, I got a job as a cook at a steakhouse in a Walmart parking lot. I cooked fried catfish and steaks and caught the bug for working in the kitchen. I stayed there all through high school, and when I was eighteen, I got a job at The Phoenician hotel in Scottsdale, Arizona. The years that I spent working there were very good training for working in high-end restaurants. I also worked as much as possible with chef Bradford Thompson at his exciting French restaurant, Mary Elaine's.

While I was in Scottsdale, I went to culinary school and met my beautiful Raquel. She and I jumped around the country together, working in fine-dining restaurants and dreaming of opening our own small place.

After a few years, I got an offer to work at the soon-to-open Alex restaurant in The Wynn Las Vegas. A friend of mine had recommended me for the job, and after a quick phone call, I received a thick package containing the recipes that I would be responsible for and a handwritten note from chef Alessandro Stratta, one of Alain Ducasse's protégés. Raquel and I moved to Las Vegas for the opening and worked for a few years with the amazing Chef Stratta at his namesake restaurant. Everything was over-the-top luxurious and the restaurant even housed an original Picasso painting. The experience of working for the chef and the team that he had built at his most ambitious stage still inspires me today.

In 2006, we moved to California so I could take a job as a sous chef at L'Auberge Carmel, a tiny restaurant that has gone on to catch the whole country's attention. The restaurant specialized in local products, and I started to learn about cooking with California's bounty and how to work directly with a farm.

On one of my first days there, a guy who looked like a surfer appeared in the kitchen with a crateful of porcini mushrooms. Instantly, I wanted to stop cooking and become a full-time mushroom hunter, selling my harvest to restaurants. I even gave it a shot, collecting chanterelles around Monterey and knocking on the back doors of restaurants on weekends. I was enamored with the idea of this guy picking mushrooms way off in the forest, which then gave me the chance to cook with them and connect the people in the restaurant to the mushrooms growing in the woods. I also realized that there might be a way to combine my love for the outdoors with my love for cooking in a restaurant that focused on using wild foods.

In 2008, I sought out a job at a small restaurant in Denmark. I scheduled a month-long stage in the kitchen at Noma with the goal of learning how a place that specialized in wild food was able to create something completely new and keep up their incredibly high standards day after day.

The kitchen under chef René Redzepi was young and fun and daring, and the food was so damn good, all using ingredients that I had never seen before. Scandinavia presented me with a whole new vocabulary of wild plants and ocean creatures like sea urchins and decades-old clams. Working there helped me define what I wanted to be doing, and the spirit I wanted to do it with. I seemed to fit in pretty well, and Chef Redzepi asked if I might be interested in sticking around a bit longer. I was! I wanted to see the food evolve through the seasons and how the menu adapted to those changes, and I simply couldn't leave while I was learning so much. I ended up staying for the next two years.

During this time, Raquel worked in some great high-end kitchens and eventually moved to the front of the house at L'Auberge Carmel. She was a natural, climbing through the ranks, and before long she was running the dining room.

We made trips back and forth between California and Denmark to see each other, but it was tough to live apart. After the second full year, I started to think of ways to reunite. From Copenhagen, I scanned Craigslist Seattle, looking for—*ahem*—an easy job, where Raquel and I could plot our next move.

Instead, I found a posting for a little inn on a tiny island in my home state that was a short ferry ride from the mainland. I didn't realize it would be more than temporary. I just thought it sounded perfect.

I sent in a résumé and started to learn a little more about the place. The owner, Riley Starks, was a real Renaissance man, and as we wrote back and forth, he told me about The Willows Inn and Lummi Island. The more I heard, the more intrigued I became. Riley started to send me pictures of his produce, of the beautiful chickens at Nettles Farm, and of the fish that he had bought from local fishermen or caught himself. We had never met, but we decided to work together and Riley even agreed to hold the position for me for another six months while I finished up in Denmark. In the meantime, he documented the twenty types of tomatoes and four kinds of potatoes he was growing, as well as the height

of the pea plants in March. I got a message from Riley's farmer a few weeks later, asking what I would like her to plant to prepare for my arrival, and Riley sent weekly updates of ingredients that were available on the island. My imagination started running wild.

Raquel and I came to Lummi Island for the first time in August 2010, taking the little ferry and looking across at the island's green mountain. I was immediately taken by the place. There was no police presence (they'll come out if you call) and no gas station, only a tiny store and

dining room, where they normally hosted about twelve guests each night. I worked alone in the kitchen, and Raquel ran the front of the house. It was a huge change from everything I'd ever done. The place was a little beat up, and I spent all of my free time those first months cleaning the kitchen and scheming about what the restaurant could become.

Much of the sense of possibility came from the instant awe that I had for the ingredients and their quality. It was a completely new level of freshness and flavor. There

lots and lots of pristine wilderness. We drove along the main road and passed some breathtaking scenery—a great bay, miles of open water, and hundreds of islands disappearing into the haze out toward the horizon.

I remember the exact moment when we drove up to The Willows for the first time. The building is perched on the edge of the ocean, and we sat on the deck and watched one of the most beautiful sunsets I had ever seen.

At the time, the Inn had a very small kitchen and

were no deliveries or ordering. Instead, we worked with what the gardener brought in that day, the fish that was caught by one of Riley's friends, and shellfish from the farm around the corner. I loved the innocence of a simple dinner that was made from what could be caught or grown nearby. It was almost impossible for me not to dream up more ambitious plans. This meant that the menu got a little longer each night and the recipes more demanding. Before long, I was enlisting anyone with a pair of hands to help me.

We certainly had early growing pains. The kitchen seemed like it had not been updated since the 1960s, and while it had some real comedic artifacts, it didn't function well. The equipment was a challenge to the point that someone needed to hold two blowtorches to the sides of a large stockpot to help the stove get hot enough to boil that much water. Coming from years of working in high-end restaurants, it was a bit of a culture shock.

But the island was amazing. My days started with a walk on the beach, collecting a few berries or herbs for get in a rowboat and pull pounds and pounds of them off the bottom of a buoy.

And every night was the most amazing sunset of my life.

In the morning, Vanessa at the front desk would hand me a sticky note with the number of diners for that night, and Raquel would help out by picking some herbs or flowers or lending a hand in the kitchen before setting up the dining room.

Things went on like this for my first summer at The

the restaurant, and then getting the kitchen going by myself. The farmer would come by for a chat and drop off the day's harvest. The ocean breeze came through the kitchen windows, and I could grab herbs from the garden right outside the door.

Amazing fish, still stiff with rigor mortis, would be dropped off at random times by a man in bright-orange foul-weather gear. Riley hunted deer, and he kept a tank full of spot prawns and Dungeness crabs just outside the kitchen. If I wanted to serve mussels, Raquel and I could

Willows, through the fall, and into the early winter. It felt perfect. We started to see an uptick in business, and November turned out to be the busiest month the Inn had ever had up to that point. Word was spreading, and we were lucky to have a lot of favorable articles written about us in the media. We started to see more people coming to the island just for the food. Just after we closed for the annual winter shutdown, we were featured in the *New York Times*. It was a lot more than I had expected.

During the winter, I convinced two friends whom

I had worked with in Denmark to join me for a while in the kitchen, Aaron Abramson and Ben Spiegel, followed shortly by a few excited chefs from the mainland. We fully remodeled the kitchen with the help of a local oven maker. Riley, a few of his friends, and I hung new ventilation hoods, and we worked all winter to get the restaurant and menu ready for the spring.

Raquel put together a great team of islanders to help her in the front of the house. She spent the winter handcrafting menu jackets out of leather from her father's farm in Paraguay, along with finding trays, silverware, and all the serving pieces for the dining room. The new energy in the dining room made diners comfortable, relaxed, and eager. Raquel pulled in the fantastic Emily Sipprell to run our little bar, Taft's, where she continues to create some of the most unique cocktails in the country. Every step of the way we were relentlessly supported by my friend and mentor, René Redzepi.

So we went for it. We spent every day trying to make great food and have fun. Things grew slowly, and we discovered more and more of the amazing ingredients on the island. Without it feeling like any time had passed, we grew into a team of more than twenty skilled and inspired people. Over time, we worked together to make what I think is an amazing restaurant in a beautiful place.

This is how we've grown from those first days, a long process that slowly defined our identity as we got to know the island. It is not our final statement on food—I am always learning, always refining. This book is an inside look at where we are right now and how we got here.

—**Blaine Wetzel**

# PROLOGUE

At a wedding in the summer of 2010, I received a lucky tip. I had just ventured two hours north of Seattle, into the land of the exotic 360 area code and up toward Canada. The urban sprawl along the highway fell away, replaced by great swaths of old-growth fir. I got off I-5 a few miles short of the border, took a left and headed toward the coast just north of Bellingham, and drove onto the *Whatcom Chief* for a short ferry ride that neatly snipped any connection with the rest of the world.

Arriving on the other side, I noticed a hand-painted sign that read "Welcome to Lummi Island," and where it once had said "Population 816," someone had penciled a line through the six and changed the number to a seven. I talked with The Willows Inn's owner, Riley Starks, at the wedding reception that evening and got a hint about who resident 817 might be.

"Well, the chef from Noma is coming here," Starks let slip, seemingly referring to René Redzepi and his groundbreaking restaurant in Copenhagen. I had little to offer in terms of a poker face, though I may have said, "Jesus. That's impossible."

The chef from Noma that Starks was talking about, however, was the *chef de partie*—a line cook with a team of several other cooks working for him—a twenty-four-year-old Washington native named Blaine Wetzel. Wetzel had started working in his first restaurant when he was fourteen, first as a dishwasher, then through every position in the kitchen. He went on to culinary school and worked in several top-shelf restaurants across the United States before his time in Europe.

This made more sense. It was the move of a young chef who could see the island's full potential and wanted to make his mark. It wasn't Copenhagen, though; Lummi Island didn't have a city full of clients who could ride their bicycles to the restaurant. By sheer virtue of its back-of-beyond-ness, Wetzel and Starks were making a huge gamble. Their client base would have to come from Seattle or Vancouver, both about two hours away, or even farther afield. Hardly an auspicious location in which to establish a thriving business, let alone a world-class restaurant. That weekend, however, Starks showed me around, and I began to realize why the young chef had chosen this spot.

In addition to running the Inn and the adjoining Nettles Farm, Starks was a commercial fisherman, meaning that, between his ventures, he could supply wonderful meat, fish, and produce to the restaurant at the Inn. Whatever he couldn't farm or fish himself was usually a phone call away to nearby farmer friends who could fill in the gaps. Not only did the Inn offer an idyllic island location, including a stunning 180-degree view of Puget Sound, it also had an unbeatable supply chain. If he brought in a strong, ambitious chef, Starks hoped he would be able to create something amazing: a world-class restaurant nestled in one of the country's most sublime regions.

I returned the following December to meet the newly arrived Blaine Wetzel, a quiet, friendly, and unassuming kid in jeans and a blue anorak. He had a boxer's crooked nose and broad shoulders. His ears stuck out, something emphasized by a close-cropped haircut, suggesting a boyishness that made me wonder if he wasn't too young to run a restaurant. My skepticism withered within thirty seconds of shaking his enormous hand and getting a sense of his hometown-kid likeability and incredible yet gentle confidence. At the tender age of twenty-four, there was already a sense of purpose and an easygoing manner.

Wetzel climbed into the Inn's beat-up Isuzu Hombre pickup, and I tagged along for the day as he picked up supplies and got to know his purveyors. As we rode the ferry and drove back roads and county highways, I found myself talking to someone who was earnest, serious, funny, and friendly. He was taking a monster leap with this restaurant in the middle of nowhere, but it was impossible not to root for him.

"We're rural. We're off the beaten path," he said, admiring his new home, still keeping his greater aspirations closer to his vest, "but the food's a different story. I'm here to define the region. For myself."

Back in the Inn's kitchen, I watched him trim the clams he'd just bought at Barlean's Fishery. He bubbled down the trimmings with wine and shallots to create a marinade for the parts he would serve, essentially supercharging their flavor.

Later, alone at my table in the busy dining room, Lummi Bay clams arrived under a sprinkle of fresh horseradish in a bowl of the marinade, now with bright-green disks of dill oil floating on top. At the very least, this was not a cuisine conceived exclusively for a rural zip code.

I tried his slow-roasted celeriac, rolled in the roasting pan to caramelize its exterior before being cut into strips and served with horseradish mousse floating on an emerald pool of thyme oil. As the courses kept coming, the artists sitting at the next table grew more and more animated. Less than a month into Wetzel's tenure and there were customers talking about the best food they had ever eaten.

Along with the clams and the celery, Wetzel served local wild mushrooms on a purée of woodruff so densely green that it looked like it had been squeezed from a paint tube; it gave the dish a primordial flavor. Slow-roasted beef cheek, from cows raised by Starks's Lummi Island farmer friend Phil Tucker ("Grass fed. That's all he does," said Wetzel), was a visceral reminder of the Inn's physical and qualitative distance from any supermarkets. Despite the young chef's modesty, this was

destination food, with clear flavors, strong technique, and beautiful presentation in a stunning place. After years of training and working his way up through great restaurants and a variety of styles, there was only one place in the world this meal could have come from. One place, and a handful of other diners and I were sitting in the middle of it, marveling at our luck.

The next morning, I met Wetzel again and pressed him on his goals.

"I went to Europe and learned how to be critical of myself and be able to really taste food. After that, I didn't want to go and work somewhere else. I wanted to run with it. I was so excited that it would have been unnatural not to try to open my own place. Plus, I don't care if you're wearing shorts and flip-flops," he said, pausing to ponder what he was about to say, "I want anyone who eats at the restaurant to have the best meal of their lives."

Wetzel may not have known it at the time, but the doubts about far-flung clients seeking out his food proved groundless. He had come to Lummi Island not knowing how long he would stay, but something bigger was brewing. He would learn the island and the bounty that was available at his fingertips. He would refine his style as a chef, and in a region that lacked a clear culinary identity, he would begin to define what the cuisine of the Pacific Northwest could be.

Two years after he arrived, the idea was no longer to serve unforgettable meals just to diners within close driving distance; people had begun to drive in from Seattle and Vancouver and to fly from across the United States and around the world to eat at the Inn. I had the chance to spend a year there, learning about the place, the chef, and the recipes that were in the process of turning The Willows Inn into one of the world's next great restaurants.

There was no way I was going to miss it.

**—Joe Ray**

# CHAPTER 1

# INTO THE KITCHEN

Three days before the annual winter shutdown at The Willows, the wind slings the flags sideways on the *Whatcom Chief* ferry. Earlier in the day, it blew hard enough to shut the ferry down for a few hours, an indication of how brutal the weather can get in Hale Passage—the narrow strait between Lummi Island and the mainland.

The next morning, it hasn't let up. The rain seems to come straight out of the sea, and a particularly high tide has submerged much of the beach on Legoe Bay, causing the tree-length timbers on shore to bob like twigs.

This is December, the month described by locals as "cold, wet, rainy, muddy, and sometimes freezing," and it is all on display on the two-mile stretch between the bay and the Inn.

Over the water to the west, a downpour drenches Clark Island and obscures Mount Constitution. On Lummi, wet leaves cover the ground and the green-brown mix in the long grass confirms that winter isn't going anywhere anytime soon. Life, however, is still rumbling along just above and below the surface. Bald eagles swirl overhead and seals poke their heads out of the water. Sheep and alpaca graze on the point occupied by Granger Ranch, where a utilitarian sign reads: "FOR SALE: Beef. Lamb. Pork." Nearer to the Inn, a welcoming whiff of smoke from their smoker reaches upwind. It's barely ten in the morning and dinner preparation is well underway.

Inside the kitchen, Blaine's team of six chefs wear black Dickies work pants instead of typical chef pants,

and many of them eschew clogs in favor of more rugged shoes that can better handle the rocky ground outdoors. Blaine checks in with Johnny, a pale, lanky twenty-something with a mop-top that makes him look like a lost member of Radiohead.

"I ran the Black Truffle Explosion station," Johnny says, by way of introduction when we meet, referring to his former role as caretaker of one of chef Grant Achatz's signature dishes.

Right now at The Willows, Johnny is doing something a bit less flashy. At his tiny station on the prep bench, sandwiched between several other cooks, he works with a pair of tweezers and a box of weeds. He's doing what this crew calls "pickin' herbs"—pulling off the tender, edible tips of the wild-growing chickweed plant that will be used as a garnish for a dish that night, and he'll spend the next few hours sifting through the box, dropping the tips into an ice bath.

The kitchen buzzes behind him: sauté pans clank, cooks sometimes trot down its length, blenders whir. It's the sound of people working in earnest, an environment where everyone is deeply focused, all day long. He keeps a timer at his station mostly to time the things he does in an effort to become more efficient.

Behind Johnny, the plancha (a.k.a. the flattop grill) sizzles away. Mikey, a scrawny cook with sandy blonde hair and the wan look of someone who never sees sunlight, fills the grill with a neat grid of onion halves, and their scent soon takes over the kitchen. While most

of each onion remains raw, the cut sides get scorched against the flattop. Mikey waits for a thick black layer of char to form before scraping the onions off the grill and disappearing with them into the prep kitchen.

The quiet neighbor to Johnny's right is Cameron, and as he fills a mixing bowl with chopped pecans, almonds, and hazelnuts, he wears an expression of something between excited confidence and total concentration.

Cameron toasts a few ultra fresh-looking bay leaves on the flattop for a moment, then reduces them to a near-powder with a square-bladed Japanese knife. While old bay leaves from a home spice rack smell like toasted cardboard when given this treatment, these fresh leaves have a complex scent like sweet and savory herbs, a completely new aroma. Sprinkled atop the warm dessert he's working on—sweet pumpkin with fresh cheese and pine—the bay will wow customers with its scent even before their first bite.

Picking the leaves may also qualify as the easiest foraging job in history for a chef and his crew. They come from a pair of ten-foot-tall bay laurel trees just outside the kitchen window, the closest living things to Cameron's station.

Two slots to the left on the prep bench, Mikey crams what looks like a crumbling handful of charred hay followed by raw scallions, shallot, and a splash of vinegar into a variable-speed Vitamix blender, a kitchen tool with a motor powerful enough to be categorized by horsepower. Blended, Mikey's project looks like thick green sludge.

"It's raw scallion and charred scallion," he says, explaining that there is also cold grapeseed oil and a bit of chicken glacé in the mix. Together, they create a thick paste that will be used with his onion dish.

Mikey grabs a spoon and dunks it into the blender. Far from tasting like charcoal, the emulsion incorporates the better qualities of the raw and the cooked. It tastes alive.

Johnny picks away at the chickweed for another half hour, coming up with a scant handful of tips, and stores them in the walk-in cooler. The chickweed now sits alongside shoebox-sized plastic bins with dated labels: mustard, thyme, lemon thyme, thyme scraps, chervil, tarragon, chives, salsify and horseradish, two containers of dill, celery, nasturtium capers in brine, a related bin simply labeled "nasty," and a tub of venison fat.

Later, in the prep kitchen, a room separated from the main kitchen by the corridor where the dishwasher works, Mikey holds bags of his charred onions, fresh from the sous vide machine, where they have poached in their own juices at a precise and relatively low temperature for a specific amount of time. The cooking leaves them pleasingly firm, but without the harsh oniony flavor.

Mikey uses a curved bird's-beak paring knife to pull the individual "shells" from the onion halves—something like extracting Russian nesting dolls from their encompassing larger sisters—yielding concentric cups with charred rims.

What he's doing is nearly as painstaking as what Johnny had done with the chickweed. He even removes the one-cell-thick "skin" between each layer of onion. That skin, which wouldn't be pleasant to eat, is hard to remove. Bits of the charred edge are prone to flaking off, meaning they'd need to be put back into place with slippery fingers. Mikey lines up neat rows of the shells on parchment-lined baking sheets, a tedious, labor-intensive job that no diner would ever realize took place.

The day begins to pass quickly, and the cooks work in a blur. Background music comes on long enough to play a Jimmy Buffett album, then goes off for the rest of the day. Every cook seems to be rotating through every job in the kitchen, right down to doing the dishes, something fairly unbelievable, considering that just about every restaurant, from cheap, backcountry diners to the Ritz in Paris, has dedicated, low-paid dishwashers.

Lunch never happens. At five, everyone breaks for the staff meal. A *stagiaire* (kitchen speak for "unpaid intern") makes burgers and a salad for the kitchen and waitstaff, and everyone eats quickly.

By 5:45, everyone is back at it in the kitchen, and at six there is a staff meeting—a quick roundup of special needs and dietary restrictions, along with a who's who of the customers, noting a few VIPs and returning diners. All of this information is also contained in the "dining report" that is taped on the table directly under the expediter's nose during dinner service.

Nine hours after everyone in the kitchen arrived for work, dinner service begins.

• • •

Part of the quality of the meals served at The Willows is a function of the restaurant's format. Dinner is a prix fixe with a set number of courses starting at a specified time. There's no à la carte dining, no showing up at nine and ordering a steak. You eat what's good, what's available and in season, and what Blaine and his team feel like making, which is almost invariably the product of days or even months of thought. This also allows them to serve only their best dishes, waste less, and concentrate more on the careful preparation of every plate.

Guests at The Willows have a cocktail on the porch overlooking the sea at about seven and are then invited into the dining room. By seating all diners within a forty-five-minute window, the kitchen can concentrate on just a few dishes at a time. Over the course of the night, six chefs can get upwards of 600 well-prepared plates out the door quickly, while maintaining exacting standards.

It makes an à la carte kitchen look like complete chaos.

On this night, seventeen courses go out of the kitchen in three hours that disappear in a flash. Entire dishes seem to appear out of the ether; it's sometimes hard to tell where they came from or who made them. Baked sunflower roots arrive on beds of moss in tiny wooden boxes that release puffs of smoke when diners open them. Sockeye salmon roe are tucked inside crisp, tube-shaped crêpes and bookended by creamy mousse and bits of chive. Fingers of salmon smoked to a near-mahogany color and covered with a translucent glaze sail out on small wooden planks. One bite through the smoky, flaky exterior reveals a texture like custard on the inside.

Surveying the kitchen over the course of the night is like watching a minutely choreographed show. The cooks huddle and work, heads down, with the quiet intensity of surgeons, talking only when they need to. Anyone who has a (rare) spare moment sets up upcoming courses in the back, helps with dishwasher duty, finds someone who needs a hand, wipes down a bench, or sweeps the floor.

When it's time to serve Mikey's onion dish, he spoons a dollop of the raw and charred scallion emulsion onto the center of each dish. Four onion "shells" of diminishing sizes, seared-edges up, are anchored on top of it. Next, Johnny balances the chickweed tips he'd picked through all morning and tiny tips of lemon thyme around the edges of the onion. The cooks spoon in warm rhubarb juice, then add a few drops of thyme oil that float like luminous disks of green atop the rosy liquid below. Chefs using tweezers to plate a dish can seem a bit fussy, but seeing this one assembled, the herbs on the rim make the onion look like it is studded with tiny jewels.

On the plate, one bite can contain multiple forms of onion: charred, raw, and supercharged with flavor, an exploration of what you can do with a single ingredient and a great deal of thought.

For the dish with aged venison and forest mushrooms,

slices of flash-cooked meat are covered with umbrella-shaped cinnamon cap mushrooms, which give the illusion of peering down on a Magritte painting. A quick-pickled fiddlehead fern sits at what would be the bottom of the painting, and a pair of wood ear mushrooms are arranged on either side. The whole thing gets a sprinkle of wild herbs.

It feels like moments after the first diners took their seats, yet it's three hours later, and Cameron takes a blowtorch to cubes of pumpkin for his dessert. Dinner is nearly done. By the time the team cleans up, they've spent almost all of the last fourteen hours on their feet. They head home, peel off their clothes, and collapse into bed. No reading, no television, no email. They have to be up in a few hours to get back to work.

• •

Even when witnessed from within, it's difficult to understand how it all happens. Where did all of those dishes materialize from? This kitchen isn't structured in the traditional top-down style most cooks are used to—the one with a very clear pecking order and a testosterone-heavy chef barking orders from the top. Here, the cooks bust their butts all day long, but understanding how it all happens, day in and day out, requires a bit of explanation.

"This isn't a traditional kitchen. It's more democratic," Nick says. "Here, each chef prepares at least one course and one snack, usually more. You do everything, start to finish, for a dish. Butchering fish, picking herbs, visiting farms, making sauces, whatever it needs."

He looks at the cooks around the kitchen and explains who is responsible for what in that night's meal. Mikey is in charge of the smoked salmon, onion, and sunchoke courses. Aaron Abramson, the other sous chef, shucks oysters, makes a crab dish, and bakes the bread. Cameron makes the pumpkin dessert with the bay leaves, the salmon roe snack Nick likes to call the "roe rolls," and another snack of crispy halibut skin studded with tiny clams. Nick himself is in charge of the venison plate and a toasted kale dish that uses the leafy green as a delivery vehicle for tiny dollops of truffle coated with tiny toasted crumbs of rye bread.

Some kitchen jobs are doled out simply based on who lives where. Johnny is the herb guy because he lives near the farm. Nick has just moved to a house along the beach, so he brings the seaweed.

"It's a collective. A cooperative. The antithesis of the French brigade mentality," he says, still conjuring up a "Three Musketeers" ethos, "but six talented minds are better than one."

As he talks, you can hear that he knows he sounds like a bit of a hippie, but Blaine's kitchen is a quiet, well-oiled machine. Nobody yells, and for the most part, nobody has to. Everyone is too busy doing their job.

Blaine's most agitated state tends to come out during a staff meeting, when he might remind everyone in the kitchen to keep it down during service, drawing and re-drawing an arrow in the margins of his notebook as he speaks. It's a rare occurrence.

"It's hard work, but it's not tense," Blaine says later. It doesn't hurt that his entire crew wants to see the restaurant succeed.

This is a kitchen full of lifers. They're the ones who are committed to the craft, appreciate the collaborative style, don't mind putting in fourteen-hour days, come to work early, and don't touch their phones all day.

In this industry, with its blisteringly high turnover rate, every cook on staff at The Willows has already signed on to come back the next year, following the annual shutdown.

"I've never been in a kitchen where we do so much positive feedback and critical analysis," Nick reflects. In his mind, the system fosters creativity. "I'll never go back to the old way."

# CHAPTER 2

## THE HANDOFF

The wild-berry hedges of Lummi Island can look like great waves frozen in midair, cresting along the roadside and engulfing whole trees. Loganita Farm in June is a managed version of that kind of fecundity, a plot where thickly packed fruit and vegetable plants swell from the ground and compete for space.

Loganita is at the northern tip of Lummi, just up West Shore Drive from the Inn, and they do nothing but grow produce for The Willows. The ocean crashes against the shore across the street, and swallows chirp and flit from fence post to tree. Above them, the sky's windblown clouds and dusty blue contrast with the hundreds of shades of green in the field.

On one of the busier San Juan Islands or over on the mainland, it would be easy to imagine real estate like this crammed with houses on view lots, but here, Loganita has a commanding view, high above the water, the neat line of the horizon taking up nearly 180 degrees, each end flanked by craggy pines favored by bald eagles on the lookout for a meal.

Both Loganita and The Willows were popular resorts throughout the 1900s, attracting hundreds of people over the course of the summer. For a time, The Willows prided itself on not serving (or tolerating) alcohol, but Loganita didn't suffer from those qualms.

Now, Loganita's garden is a smart, spare production. It's a half acre delineated by a tall fence made of wood and wire with a simple shed near the gate. Along one of the rectangle's long sides, four plastic greenhouses—known

around here as hoop houses—amp up the heat. In the middle of summer, they fill with the smell of tomato plants, bringing immediately to mind your dad's garden when you were a kid. Nearby, sixteen raised beds are followed by row after long row of crops. Depending on the vantage point on the farm's gently sloping hill, the plot can feel either slight or intensely abundant. It is simple, elegant, and functional.

The shed, exponentially neater and more sparse than most backyard sheds, contains a minimal amount of typical garden gear with shovels, pitchforks, rakes, a few tubs of seeds, and an 8,000-foot spool of watering hose known as T-tape.

A casual observer strolling the farm will see flowers and plants like tomato starts in the greenhouses, along with lettuce and strawberries. An avid gardener will spot the kale, kohlrabi, and tomatillos, along with unusual versions of plants like the red-speckled Trout's Back lettuce and Caraflex cabbage.

The gardener here is Mary von Krusenstiern. Mary is Blaine's age, and she lopes around Loganita's raised beds barefoot when it's nice out and sports rubber fishing boots when it's not.

While home gardening tends to focus on using fertilizer to nourish the plant, here, Mary concentrates on feeding the soil.

"All organic fertilizer uses microbes to break down the soil and soil nutrients to make them available to the plant, and that needs a certain amount of heat," she says, working some fertilizer into the soil with her hands as she talks and explaining the relatively slow start to the growing season in the Pacific Northwest. "Synthetic fertilizer comes from a lab. This stuff comes from a chicken's butt."

That mentality yields healthier plants that can better repel pests and disease.

"Most veg has traveled an average of 1,000 miles. Apples come from New Zealand. I guarantee you that the greens in the grocery store are already two or three weeks old by the time you buy them," Mary says matter of factly, before playing her trump card. "Here, we can harvest and deliver on the same day."

What this yields on the palate, particularly those of city dwellers or those who have never grown a backyard garden, is extraordinary. Blaine talks about "juicy food" like it's something the supermarket-bound world understands, but in reality, nothing like this ever hits the shelves at the local Safeway.

This is easy to understand when walking across Loganita's field and nibbling whatever is close at hand. While something like store-bought broccoli rabe can be intensely bitter, here it bursts with a not-too-strong flavor. Kohlrabi, which can send people scurrying to a cookbook to figure out what to do with it, can be peeled with a pocketknife and chomped like a carrot. When the big gray tubs of rainbow chard that Mary delivers in the farm's pickup are opened at the Inn, the

two- to three-foot leaves burst from the box, their stems saturated in color, the whole thing looking like a prop from the set of Land of the Lost.

Mary was born and raised in Bellingham, coming to her family's camp on Lummi for weeks, weekends, and holidays as she grew up, the island framing her personality. She's an outdoorsy person who can get a little twitchy at a dinner party and, in recent years, has returned to live in the house in Bellingham where she was raised.

Her path to farming might sound peculiar, but it's also straight as a string.

Fresh out of high school in 2002, she spent five months hiking the Pacific Crest Trail, top to bottom. All 2,663 miles of it. All by herself. Then she went to Europe to travel, picking strawberries in Germany whenever the money ran out.

In college, she spent much of her time developing the agroecology internship program between Lesley University's Audubon Expedition Institute and Calypso Farm and Ecology Center in Ester, Alaska.

"With the Expedition Institute, you drive around in an old school bus to different bioregions," she explains. "There's a library in the back and all of our stuff was on top."

When the bus stopped in Ester for a few weeks in the fall of 2004, it was her formal introduction to small-scale organic farming. Mary returned the following spring and stayed for six months, the first intern in the program she'd helped to create.

She came back home, then followed a boyfriend to Keene, New Hampshire, where she finished her degree. They lived in a yurt next to a vacant building, followed by another yurt on his parents' land. It really didn't matter to them. They just wanted to farm.

"Right before we started, the farmer who had hired us told us he could only pay us six dollars an hour, so we decided to expand our backyard into a farm and started selling at the farmers' market," she says. "So we planted strawberries and asparagus in a field away from the house and had no idea how we'd water them."

They'd go to the farmers' market with an onion, two tomatoes, and a card table. They raised turkeys and chickens and killed them by hand, and slowly, they started gaining a following.

"We didn't care. We were driven. We wanted to make it happen, and we didn't care about the rest."

When she moved back to Washington, Mary worked at Sunseed Farm in Acme for a few years, then started farm on leased land in Bellingham. She built hoop houses, buying straight metal tubing at Home Depot and bending it to make the roof frame. She borrowed a broken tractor to till the land and figured out how to fix the steering box by herself in a friend's machine shop.

"Farming is a love-hate relationship that bypasses a lot of people," she says. "Every year, it gets better. Every year, you learn more. Every year it gets a little easier."

Easier, but still all-consuming. She worked the fields and ran the business of the farm twelve hours a day, seven days a week, and eventually, she burnt out.

In 2013, Mary was skimming through the Whatcom Farmers' Google Group, a listing of what she calls "job postings, tractors for sale, and people with extra onions," when she came across a promising lead out on Lummi Island.

Flash forward and there she is, loping around barefoot in June, the ground around her tightly packed with leafy green plants and bursting with more produce than it seems could possibly come out of the tiny plot. Different lettuce varieties crowd up, nine heads per square foot, a thick carpet of green and red pushing above the bed; they are a product of the years she's spent in the Pacific Northwest, figuring out what works well and how to coax them along.

That crowding is by plan. Mary often double plants

the seeds, which are relatively cheap, to make sure something grows. When a planting is harvested for the last time, the roots are tossed into the compost heap and the space is immediately replanted.

"We plan for disaster, and we use several varieties in case something goes wrong. One type might get a disease that another won't, one variety might take longer to germinate than another. We always need more to..." she trails off in the thought for a moment before returning to clarify. "We always need more."

The goal, it turns out, is to close the circuit and have the ability to deliver 100 percent of the produce for every day the restaurant is open.

She even plants 20 percent more than the Inn will need, so if bad things happen, she has plenty to show for her efforts.

"I don't think there isn't a week that goes by where we don't plant something," she says, gesturing toward the rows in front of her. "Two weeks from now, this'll look totally different."

Blaine and Mary learned to take an adaptive approach to get the farm and the Inn working together. There was a good deal of trial and error in the early days as Mary figured out what grew, what didn't, and how the year's weather would play out, versus what Blaine wanted, needed, and wished to explore. It's still a process that requires give and take, something that is much more difficult than calling Charlie's Produce in Seattle, but there's no need to worry about quality, freshness, or provenance. It's all juicy. It produces miraculous results.

"Ingredient quality is the key. A roasted head of lettuce could be ordinary, but here, it's amazing. I can go after harvesting dates and work to get unique products. I can get tiny escarole, then escarole flowers and escarole seeds. My one ingredient turns into ten throughout the season. Plus, I can walk around tasting things. If I know what's wild and what's being caught, I can walk around

the farm and know what will be perfect with that night's fish course," Blaine says. He's not bound by what he can buy commercially, what stores well, or what ships the best. "I can just go after flavor. It's huge. When a chef's working directly with their farm, all of a sudden, they're amazed by a potato."

The farm gives him unique ingredients that he chooses, the kind of stuff that people would be hard-pressed to find at the market or at another restaurant.

None of this would work if the Inn were a bigger restaurant.

"We've got a temperate climate here that allows for a huge amount of flexibility. December is a full farm. The crops we plant late in the year mean that when we come back after winter break in March, we have a full farm then, too," he says. "It's no July, but with only thirty covers a night, we can still run a full menu on Loganita produce."

There's also a functional side to having a farm on Lummi.

"Having a farm for The Willows has been practical since before I got here. We're on an island. It's rural. It's hard to cart things back and forth from the mainland," he says. "This is part of our foundation."

For his part, Blaine is constantly figuring out what he can get and what Mary can grow, and there's a balance to strike between the time it takes to create a dish and the limited seasonality of its ingredients. This leads to conversations at the farm between him and Mary that start with, "I've got a lotta zucchini," and, "Too many turnips next week might cramp my style," or, "The fennel's here...I'm just not there yet."

On an overcast morning in late June, the two of them walk down the rows with Willows cook Kyle Bartholomew, and Mary gives the chefs a running update on what she's got, what's running low, and what she'll have soon, with Blaine munching, calculating, and asking questions. He pauses to examine the flowers and the peculiarly thin-fingered leaves from a patch of coriander plants that have begun to bolt.

"I like that they're different—that they make people notice what they're eating," he says.

Further into the rows, a visible glut of turnips and peas is a bit of a dilemma, as Blaine's dishes that feature those ingredients are too similar for his taste.

"I'll have to come up with a new pea dish," he decides.

He pushes Mary for early-season strawberries—200 a day—a number that makes her cringe when she does the math. They settle on an even hundred.

Behind them trails Kyle, who, when he first came to Lummi, was wide-eyed over the farm and the quantity of food it could produce.

"The restaurant I worked at in Colorado Springs

bought a corner of the community garden to use. It was more of an experiment than something dependable for the restaurant, but when it worked, it was good for our egos," he says. "When I first came to Lummi, I was amazed by Loganita, but now I can't imagine cooking any other way."

They head toward the back of the garden, where Blaine bends over, pushes back the canopy of zucchini leaves with his red Moleskine notebook, and stares at the perfect vegetables, some a deep Pantone green, others a blazing yellow.

He frowns.

"These look like the supermarket variety," he says.

If someone's flying in for a world-class dinner, he's got a point.

Undeterred, Mary reaches down to the base of a plant

SEA AND SMOKE

and lifts out a four-inch yellow zucchini crowned by a flower that resembles a frozen flame.

"How about this?" she asks.

Blaine's eyes light up, and as they talk, he sets down his red notebook on the wooden workbench, with the flower, a tiny bunch of basil, and some frilly-edged lettuce arranged on top of it, as if he's already testing plating ideas.

Back in the kitchen five minutes later, he's at his station with the same zucchini flower, now cut in half lengthwise and flashed gently on the flattop with a bit of clarified butter.

He pulls out a service plate and puts half of a crookneck squash across one edge and stares at it, thinking.

There's a stark contrast between the saturation of the vegetable and the earth tones of the speckled gray dish, and Blaine arranges the flower so that it looks like a blaze of color across the plate.

He stares some more, then grabs some tiny pistou basil tips, each no larger than a fingernail, and arranges them on top of the flower.

He takes one last look at the unfinished dish, then pulls out his spoon and tastes.

"I like to taste the main ingredients first," he says, "then I'll work on the dish."

He sets out spoons for the other cooks so he can gather some opinions—A bit too much butter? A pinch of flake salt? Less basil?—and gets to work in earnest, pulling out everything he needs: a box of nasturtium flowers along with some of the plant's leaves and stems, apple cider vinegar, some lovage oil, a bucket of ice, and a blender.

Riffing on a recipe for watercress sauce, he makes a sauce from the nasturtium flowers, keeping the ingredients cold to thicken the sauce since there's no emulsifier to help hold it together.

What emerges is pumpkin colored, all of the nasturtium's yellows, oranges, and deep reds blended to create something with a tingly, vivid flavor. It will become the sleeper element of the dish.

He pours a bit of the purée into a small saucepan, adds some deep green lovage oil, and gives it just enough of a stir to swirl the colors around each other. It's dramatic in the pan, but on a shallow dinner plate it doesn't work; the colors bleed together.

Blaine stares, taps his fingers on the cutting board, then grabs a shallow bowl and makes a circle with the oil, spooning the unadulterated flower purée into the center. The green ring expands, hemmed in by the rise of the bowl's edge, making a perfect circle around the nasturtium sauce.

The zucchini flower reappears, is rotated, flipped, and moved toward the side of the dish. Two wedges of squash are set across the plate lengthwise, are removed, and return again. Blaine places a finger of roasted pink salmon on the dish at an angle. Nasturtium petals and a few of its tiny, disk-shaped leaves are used as a garnish but look as if they'd grown right there, next to a few flecks of basil.

The dish goes on the menu that night. It changes and evolves over the next few days, eventually becoming roast squash, raw blossoms, nasturtium sauce, nasturtium leaves, lovage oil, and lovage salt. It's elaborated on by being pared down, an extension of the farm, its bounty and its restrictions, a distillation of the farm on the plate.

From here on out, Kyle stops at the farm to pick up the zucchini flowers every day on his way to work.

## CHAPTER 3

# CAUGHT

A mile south of the Inn, the road arcs off to the left to follow the shore along Legoe Bay. It's a spot where you might think you'd lose the sweeping views of the sound, but on a sunny day, Mount Baker looms above the island, a stunning first view of the American continent.

On shore, a seawall protects the road at the point where it abuts the stony beach. On the inland side is the Granger farmland, where heifers and their calves roam a field that starts along the shore and extends up into the trees. About 100 feet into the field is a swath of rocks and small logs that have been thrown over the seawall, across the street, and into the meadow by storms that tear up Rosario Strait from the south.

Out in the bay, the current and wind rip against each other to twist lines of foam on the water's surface for hundreds of feet at a stretch. The push and pull of the tide brings silt up from the bottom, making the water lighter in color farther out, where the tug of the current makes gentle rollers look like they're moving in slow motion.

Thousands of logs—fallen trees from up and down the coast and escapees from log booms—barkless and bleached near-white by the sun, sit above the high tide line on the beach. Occasionally, a particularly high tide reaches up and reclaims a log, sending it pitchpoling horizontally down the shoreline. Out in deeper water, the tips of floating logs known as "deadheads" poke out of the water and keep sailors honest.

From the beach, the sound of splashing fish will likely precede the first sighting of salmon—sockeye, pink, coho, Chinook, and chum—on their way north to spawn. *Plouf! Plouf!* In twos and threes come sounds like big tubes of salami being lobbed into the water, jumps that some say are a preparation for the upriver run ahead.

It's right here, among the tendrils of the bay's tide swirls, that for a few months starting in the late summer, fishing boats known as gears are anchored into place to set up for a centuries-old method of fishing called reefnetting.

The salmon that the fishermen here hope to catch start their lives in and around Canada's Fraser River, which empties into the Strait of Georgia about forty miles to the north. From there, they tend to move west, out into what's known as "the gyre," the migratory pattern that brings them into the Bering Sea. Depending on the species, they'll begin their return to the Fraser two to three years later, heading east until they hit land, then either north or south to the Fraser, fattening themselves up on krill, zooplankton, and small fish.

That fattening is key to flavorful fish. "The Fraser salmon has some of the highest fat content among any salmon in the world," says the Inn's former owner, Riley Starks, the *éminence grise* of reefnetting and one of the owners of Lummi Island Wild, the fishing outfit that holds one of the eleven permits now issued to reefnetters in the San Juans. "Some of the fish still have 1,500 miles of river to navigate to get back to where they came from in the Fraser and its tributaries."

The most particular thing about reefnet fishing is that the gears (boats) don't move. The basics of the technique were developed by Native Americans on the greater Salish Sea, and Lummi Island became a well-known spot to reliably catch fish. Today, any power the gears use comes from car batteries, and many of those are charged with solar panels on the gears themselves. The only fossil fuels consumed are those used by the skiffs that ferry the crew back and forth and for the tenders that transport the fish to the processor. It's a method that's been oddly unaffected by technological advances. "Really, the major technology change was polarized sunglasses," says Starks, referring to a 1936 innovation that cuts down on surface glare, allowing fishermen to better peer into the depths. "Other than that, a native from hundreds of years ago would still recognize the fishery."

The setup for reefnetting involves a pair of gears anchored parallel to each other a few hundred feet offshore, where they sit for the season. Each bow and stern has a lookout tower, which swing like metronomes above the port and starboard sides, slowly marking time to the waves below. Seen from shore, the men in the lookouts appear to float in midair.

The crew is a thick-skinned bunch, and when they're not in Legoe Bay, they might be working the fisheries in Alaska or Antarctica, or sitting in a university classroom. They arrive before the season's scheduled start, wait as long as a month for the Pacific Salmon Commission to declare the season open, and live in shacks and out of the backs of their cars on Legoe Bay.

They work hard, smoke aggressively, shower infrequently, drink, and cuss. They like to brag about things like working fifty-six consecutive hours on a Dungeness crab boat off the Oregon coast before stopping to take a catnap in a crab pot in their foul-weather gear. Most of all, they dream of the big score: catching enough fish in a season—100,000 pounds—to participate in the local custom of flying an upside-down broom like a flag atop one of the watchtowers.

Despite its rickety appearance, reefnetting is extremely efficient at catching salmon when the fish ride a flood tide north. A set of cables festooned with plastic streamers stretches out from the front of each pair of gears and down to the ocean floor like a scoop shovel, spooking the fish toward the bunt—the net that's strung between the boats.

Once caught, a process that takes one hectic minute, the fish go from the bunt, over the gunwale, and into a livewell—in this case, a hole in the boat's floor with a net beneath it, allowing the fish to go directly back into the water they just came from. The fish swim in the livewell, allowing any lactic acid that's accumulated in the struggle to dissipate. Bycatch like flounder, along with protected species like Chinook and coho, are flipped back into the drink, unharmed.

"Every time you handle a fish, it degrades it a little bit. These fish are handled once, then they get set on slush ice and that's where they stay until they get processed," Starks says. "The main reason we do this kind of fishing is for the quality of the fish. I got into it because I could put better fish in my freezer."

From the top of the tower closest to the Rosario Strait, gear boss Ian Kirouac calls the plays on one of Lummi Island Wild's gears. Ian is fit, on the edge of wiry, and on sunny days in season, he wears a big, bushy beard, a long-sleeve T-shirt, oversized polarized sunglasses, a ball cap, and an industrial-grade trio of muck boots, waterproof bib pants, and bright-orange rubber gloves.

Ian spends huge hunks of the day with his back to the sun, hands shielding the sides of his face to keep the glare out, his head down, watching for the fish to come up toward the surface between the gears.

From the lookout tower, Ian is so quiet it's initially hard to tell if fish are coming in at all. When they appear, the school is like a notion or a trick of the light on the water. Ian quietly winds his right leg around the metal pole at the top of his tower, leans into the railing, takes hold of a cord attached to a winch with one hand, and raises the other in the air. Any chatter among the crew dies out at this point.

Below him, a school of salmon—dozens of fish—emerges from the spindly refractions of sunlight in the water, moving into the space between the two gears.

Ian drops the hammer with one word.

"Go!"

The wiry Texan on the rear tower who acts as the crew's enforcer is much less subtle.

"Do it! Do it! Now! Now! *Now!*"

At this point, no matter how much the crew has prepared, all hell breaks loose. Winches scream, snatching up the slack in their lines before yanking the boats hard, causing the lookout towers to swing wildly.

The fish make a sharp U-turn when they come up to the back of the bunt, and from his tower at the front of

the boat, Ian makes full-arm claps, accented by his huge orange gloves, to spook the fish back into the net.

The winches at the ends of each boat are still spinning. On Ian's gear, they're World War II bomb bay door winches and they scream like circular saws cutting through sheet metal, whipping cables taut and drawing the boats closer together until the headrope at the front of the net broaches. The fight is only beginning, but once that line comes out of the water, the lives of the fish have effectively ended.

With the gears pulled close, the confines of the net concentrate everything in one space—an ever-tightening knot of writhing, panicking fish, spraying water into the air. Ian has flown down the tower's ladder, and he and every crew member funnel that mass of fish toward the livewell below the main boat's deck. As the crew claws the net in a mad, hand-over-hand rush, foot-wide purple jellyfish roll down its length, residual bits of their tentacles leaving everyone with itchy patches of goose bump-like welts on their forearms.

Still trapped, the knot of fish is pulled into a tight ball in the remaining slack of the net. With a prolonged heave, the crew pulls the last of the net out of the water, sending the fish sliding across a small deck—a mass so dense that it obscures their feet—and straight into the livewell. Along their backs, the fish have blue and green coloring so bright that it borders on fluorescence, only taking on the silvery hues we see at the grocery store once they're on ice.

Before the last fish is out of the net, Ian is back up on the tower, slacking the lines and putting the gears back into place. When the fish are running, any time that the net is out of the water, money is swimming away.

On deck, the work intensifies. The deckhands get on their knees around the livewell, then reach in with one hand and, with a practiced gesture recalling a Vulcan nerve pinch, immobilize a fish by grabbing it just behind the gill plates, pluck it from the water, and quickly pull the end of a gill free with the other hand. The fish is flipped into a second livewell, where a crimson puff of blood marks each heartbeat as the fish calmly swims from one life into the next.

Counting the fish as they go, the crew does this vigorous, jerking work in a spray of blood, scales, and saltwater that covers their bibs, gets in their hair, and dries on their faces. For all the calm there can be on a quiet day, this is grueling, intensely physical work that taxes even a young body. They yell at each other, barking like dogs when it gets busy and things go awry.

"Remember, guys, we're not out here for fun," howls the Texan, as the crew works to process a catch. "We're out here to get rich! The kind of rich where you can get fancy cigarettes and good booze!"

When the skiff—the twenty-foot aluminum boat used to ferry the crew and their catch—is loaded, it moves slowly, so weighed down that the tip of the bow sits lower than the top of the transom. The skiff drivers tend to be younger guys who often drive standing at the stern, surfing the boat like an extension of their body. Ian is back up in the tower and watching, gloved hands shielding the sides of his face, leaning in toward the water, waiting to call the next haul.

"I like how reefnetting is place dependent: you learn a spot. You have to observe it through every tide, watch the currents, watch how the fish move, watch the wind and the weather," says Starks. "It's not about catching the most fish; the whole idea is catching everything that comes your way. I'd been fishing all my life when I started reefnetting, and it still took me five years to understand how it really works. It's hard, inefficient, and labor-intensive. You wouldn't call it a popular way to catch fish, but if it ever gets to the point where the runs are depleted, reefnetting will be the one that stays."

# CHAPTER 4

## FIRST HARVEST

In late spring, an e-mail went out to a group of The Willows' customers announcing the First Harvest Dinner, the Inn's annual event in which visiting chefs spend a day on the island learning what they've got to work with, then come together to create a two-night-only menu.

The event sold out in thirty minutes.

At eleven in the morning on a Tuesday in July—one day before they're to start working together in the kitchen—the five chefs who have just flown in from across the country and around the world meet on the farm.

Mary is in on her day off. For weeks, she and her helper Chelsea have been planning for the chefs' arrival, not knowing exactly what they would want or need, but with summer's peak approaching, the bounty the chefs are walking into is unbelievable, a full snapshot of the season.

A visiting chef would be thrilled to walk into this setup.

In their civvies, the chefs look like they're part of a rock band. Grant Achatz, from Chicago's high-concept Alinea restaurant, wears John Lennon–style sunglasses. Dominique Crenn, of San Francisco's Atelier Crenn, has a flop of hair and a leather jacket that make her look like a female member of The Strokes. Virgilio Martínez, of Central restaurant in Lima, Peru, is a high-voiced former pro skater. Christopher Kostow, from Napa's The Restaurant at Meadowood, sports a scruffy beard and thick-framed glasses that give off a touch of "bad boy in the back of the bus" vibe. Justin Yu, from Houston's

Oxheart, trails quietly after everyone, taking it all in.

For his part, Blaine plays host, showing his guests the island and sharing his restaurant with them. It's his job to inspire his visitors, showcasing everything the island has to offer.

After their long flights, the chefs wander around the farm like the kids with the golden tickets at Willy Wonka's factory, and they immediately begin snapping off tastes of whatever fruit, flower, or leaf is nearest.

The first cherry tomatoes of the season have arrived, bright orange and deep red, the plants strung up to pipes in four hoop houses. Beneath them are carpets of basil—green, green with violet buds, and the tiny-leafed pistou variety—taking up all of the ground-level space in the garden beds.

Strawberries still grow in the semi-shade between the hoop houses, while the raspberries keep pushing into summer, and in bed seven, heads of Caraflex cabbage sprout up like giant cigars, unraveling as they grow.

In the ground beds farther back, the bluish leaves of leeks flop over on themselves atop their bright-white stalks, thick as a baby's wrist.

Of course, there's more: cabbage and kale, dill, and head upon head of different types of lettuce and radicchio. To the very back grow tender green beans so young and light, they curl skyward to grow, not yet encumbered by their own weight.

Chef Achatz and his number-two, Eric Rivera, wander off on their own, conferring near-telepathically with nods, raised eyebrows, and cocks of the head. Chef Martínez is still in a daze from the long-haul flight from Lima.

Chef Crenn thinks out loud, quietly articulating a concept that has yet to be fully formed. "A fumet. Pudding with olive oil and vinegar and chervil. Gooseberries," she says, perhaps describing different elements on one plate, "seaweed, foie gras, and crustacean" on another. She sketches a squared-off plate in her notebook, with pea shoots making little curlicues in one corner of a dish.

"What's this?" Chef Kostow asks Mary, holding out a flower at the end of a row.

"That's the only inedible thing out here," she replies.

"Hmm," he says. "I think I'll do a pork dish."

Chef Yu has better luck. It's the tail end of raspberry season and after a lap around the garden, he returns to the bushes along the fence on the garden's southern edge.

"I'm thinking about raw raspberries. Maybe lightly salted. With liquefied kale and cucumber, and sunflower and cilantro flowers," he says, already comparing the flavors in his mind. "Acidic and savory. Toward the beginning of the meal."

It's surprisingly close to the dish he'll end up serving.

After twenty minutes, Mary tears a cardboard box into a twelve-by-twelve square, grabs a marker, and announces that she's ready to take orders.

Chef Rivera walks right up to her. He and Chef Achatz would like pea tendrils, a hundred baby cucumber flowers—"about an inch long, including the flower and the cuke"—a hundred kale flowers, fifty large leeks, two gold and two brown sunflowers, twenty cilantro flower bunches, and large quantities of basil-flower tips. "Just the tips," he says.

All orders in, the group leaves Loganita and heads up the hill to see Riley Starks at Nettles Farm. Chef Crenn is enamored of a little flock of chickens that remind her of

the famous *poulet de Bresse* from her native Brittany. She snaps photos as she goes. Chefs Achatz and Rivera grab handfuls of micro-sized grape bunches.

Later, everyone hops into waiting Zodiac boats to take them to the uninhabited southern end of the island. On the eastern side, just south of the island's quarry, they pull up to a tidal flat where oysters and large purple starfish dot the shore, looking like they've been poured onto the rocks. Chefs Achatz and Rivera disappear in search of something under the overhang of trees above the high tide line. Chef Yu drops to his knees on the muddy sand, pulls out a pair of work gloves with "TEXAS" printed on the cuff, and starts digging for clams.

"*Il y a des moules!*" cries Chef Crenn. There *are* mussels—another Breton specialty—tight clusters of them, each one smaller than a thumb and covered with barnacles. She mentions something about a broth, then skitters away.

Chef Kostow reaches into the water, pulls up long fronds of seaweed, and appears happy.

"I'll smoke the pork inside this and tie it off with eelgrass," he says matter of factly.

Chefs Achatz and Rivera reappear toting plastic boxes full of rocks, lichen plucked from the trees above the shore, and a section of bull kelp. They resume their clipped dialogue.

"Crab salad in cross sections of bull, pluche of lichen. Color from ground-up soft sections of crab shell," one says.

"We just need to make sure the crab salad has some acid," the other replies.

They both nod and walk their bins to the boat.

At a beach on the western side of Lummi, Blaine notices a fat squirt of water shoot out of the sand at the water's edge.

"Give me the shovel," he says.

Moving quickly, he digs into the muddy sand a few

inches behind the hole, clears out a bucket-sized space, and drops to his knees, plunging his hands into the muck as if diving after whatever's down there. He moves his arms as if trying to pry out a heavy, moving object.

"Geoduck," he declares, not looking up. "They're fast."

Raquel, who has joined the group for this part of the day, moves in next to him, clearing sand and rocks. This is clearly not the first time they've done this. There's a deep sucking sound, and together they pull up a softball-sized bivalve, its trademark neck drawn up toward the shell.

Everyone gathers around them in a circle, and they let out a collective gasp. There's a look on their faces like they're amazed that more of these could be beneath their feet. Perhaps inspired, Chef Martínez spends the next half hour artfully coaxing geoduck and other bivalves to the surface, flipping them into his bucket.

And that's it. Now it's late afternoon and that's all the time they have to come up with dishes that represent their skill and style. That night, before they have a meal as guests of The Willows, all the chefs meet in the private dining room.

"So, what do you want to cook?" Blaine asks the group, listing each dish in his notebook. They quickly determine the best order in which to serve everything, and Blaine puts a number next to each course. "Easy as that," he says.

• • •

The next morning, there's an air of congeniality as the chefs continue to get to know one another, but there's also a whiff of friendly competition. The next two nights will not be like when Chef Crenn was on *Top Chef* and *Iron Chef America*—but every diner who has traveled to be here hopes and expects to get a taste of each chef at their best, even if the chefs are being thrown into an unfamiliar circumstance. As Chef Kostow puts it, "There's a huge possibility for catastrophe. You don't want to be the guy who made the dish that sucked."

No visiting chef is walking around on eggshells while they're here, however. On the contrary, there's a spirit of camaraderie and inspiration, yet each one uses the event to push themselves to create new food.

"It's a challenge to cook with and keep up with this caliber of chefs. You all take the same product and come at it from a different angle," says Chef Yu, whose angle is sticking to his guns. "I can't out-cook these guys, so I try to stick with some very specific flavors. I go for all-out simplicity."

Chef Crenn has come for a chance to spread her wings and get to know her peers.

"You usually get inspiration from other chefs by reading about what they're up to in the newspaper," she says. "It's more challenging and rewarding when you cook everything around you. You're so happy to be in surroundings that create a dialogue between chefs. This is a chance for us to see where we are in our lives."

In a First Harvest diner's eyes, anyone who cooks at a dinner here and knocks it out of the park transforms his or her own restaurant from what might have been an abstract concept into a must-visit destination. Taste the right food by Chefs Kostow and Crenn, and somebody starts talking about taking a trip to the Bay Area. Trips to Alinea and Peru go on the bucket list.

Blaine's motivation for hosting the event is slightly different.

"This is our party for the whole year. I get to work with chefs that I admire and share all the exciting things we're doing with them. Plus, they share their ideas with our team. Everybody here is invigorated because they get to work with people who treat the same ingredients we do in a totally different way. They come out of it completely inspired," he says. "Plus, it encourages everyone who comes here to work even harder when we see someone like Chef Achatz here. He's a total badass and he's not sitting back."

In the end, Chef Achatz used the event as a new way to challenge himself.

"It's a different kind of pressure. Usually we prep for an event like this in Chicago. At home we're methodically organized, but we didn't know what was available here, so we couldn't do that. At Alinea, it takes months or a year to come up with a dish or a technique, so this is very different for us. Not better or worse, just different," he says, snipping coriander flowers into a container the whole time he's talking. "It's impressive to walk around the garden. I wish we could do that back home."

· ● ·

During the day, the kitchen is crowded and the atmosphere intense. The visiting chefs are working with people they've only just met, sharing a kitchen they've never before set foot in, and cooking a meal they've only just conceived, which will be served to diners who are fully expecting the best meal of their lives.

Each member of The Willows' kitchen staff has been paired up with a visiting chef—"We spun a Sharpie, 'spin the bottle' style," Blaine explains—a fantastic opportunity for his staff to learn. Chefs Achatz and Rivera showed up three hours early, and everyone is deeply concentrated and almost silent, save the occasional French-style gasped "Oui!"

In the late morning, Chef Kostow's wife, Martina, takes two steps into the kitchen, pivots, and walks right back out again, saying, "Veeeery serious."

Austin, a friend of Blaine and Aaron's and a sous chef at an acclaimed New York City restaurant, has taken the week off and flown in to work the kitchen for the event. When he first appears, he's running a vacuum through the back kitchen and preparing for a bit of dish duty.

Asked what he's doing here, he grins. "Dishes for now. I'm sure I'll give somebody a hand, but for now I'm going to run the tightest dish pass in the world."

Blaine, who's both conducting this symphony and cooking his own dishes, shows Chef Crenn how to pull live spot prawns from the tank next to the kitchen. She promptly pops a net's worth into a metal tray, then puts the whole thing in the blast freezer to make them easier to peel. Chef Achatz peels the outer skin from rainbow chard stems, and Chef Rivera creates long shavings from broccoli stems. Chef Martínez, wearing skinny jeans, funky striped socks, and Birkenstock sandals, glides through the kitchen with a pair of squeeze bottles filled with a bubble-gum-pink liquid. Cameron heads in the other direction, smelling as if he were made of mint. Nick plucks a pair of Dungeness crabs from the tank next to the prawns, dispatches them with the tip of a chef's knife, and tosses them on the grill.

At four, Chef Achatz chugs a Diet Coke, and at five, Blaine calls a quick meeting to go over last-minute details. Everyone wolfs a staff meal at six because dinner starts at seven, at which point the real show begins.

· ● ·

When the seating starts, the waitstaff begins to occupy their space in the kitchen around the pass. There are times when, with the chefs in white and the front-of-house staff in black, it resembles high-speed chess, occasionally prompting Blaine to ask any nonessential staff to wait on the porch until they're needed, as a way to keep things in order.

Back in the prep kitchen, everyone darts around like they're on cocaine. A stagiaire peels a carrot in a heartbeat, and Chef Crenn charges through with knitted eyebrows, saying only, "We fucked up," before disappearing around the corner. Chef Achatz accidentally jams his knuckles on the walk-in door. Blaine walks out to the porch, opens a broken cooler that turns out to be full of bottles of frozen Champagne, and asks how this could have happened to no one in particular. Above his head, the electric meter whizzes around fast enough that the dial could almost hover, and inside, the ice machines at full tilt. The freezer compressor has blown out, meaning the guys in the back get to step over the repairman, and while he's there, the old, five-door reach-in cooler gives up the ghost. Every chef in here has encountered problems like these in the past. Nobody bats an eye.

Aaron's in the expediter's slot when things really get moving. His job is to track where in the meal each of the forty diners is at any given point and to keep things running smoothly. He looks down at the sheet taped below his nose and can tell whether or not their most recent dish has been cleared from any given table and reset with new silverware. He makes sure wine glasses are full and checks if one of his chefs is ready to start plating forty dishes in a semi-staggered rush. Over the course of the evening, he also needs to make sure that every chef visits each table at least once. So many more people, new faces, and additional details make an exponential shift in organization up from a "normal" full house at the Inn, and there was no way to do a trial run. It's a big, beautiful thing they're doing, but it's also a train that could go off the rails without everyone's complete attention.

At eight, Aaron hits top speed. If he were to miss a step, the whole service would go down with him, something no one could step in and fix. At the night's busiest moment, he pauses, examines the dining chart,

pivots to his left to check in with Raquel, and squeaks out dishes for a pair of two-tops, scooting them up in the line in order to clear out space for the dishes for a pair of larger tables, which, once they're out, will allow for smooth sailing into the heart of the dinner service. Once he knows he's in the clear, he thrusts his fist into the air, pumps it three times, and grins larger than seems possible, then gets right back to work.

Outside, Chef Crenn has the porch to herself and begins plating her next course, which centers around spot prawns and venison. She does it alone, speaking a pleasant mix of French and English to herself. She blitzes a cream-colored liquid with an immersion blender, creating a cool, airy mousse that releases a scent that could be worn like perfume.

"Taste," she says, offering a spoonful to Nick.

It has an almost creamy texture and a pure taste of the sea that, instead of disappearing quickly, lingers on the tongue. She knows it's liquid gold and that it's hard to guess exactly what it's made from.

"*C'est du foie gras et des moules,*" she says giddily: foie gras she'd special ordered, with local mussels.

"Ah, you're cheating!" he says.

"No, I'm French!" she exclaims, savoring another bite. "Mmm, those mussels. *C'est comme en Bretagne.*"

Here, on an island nine time zones west of France, she's found what she needs to remind herself of home.

Now, she pieces her dish together, and she does it by herself, taking her time, nibbling, thinking, enjoying the space she's carved out for herself on the porch. In San Francisco, she needs to keep an eye on every dish, the expediting, the customers, her staff, everything. Here, she can worry about just one course and take the time to challenge herself and make it perfect.

"I'm here. I want to cook. I don't want to do stuff I've done before," she says, taking the liberty to be an artist, grooving on the knowledge that she's making something

good. She takes a taste of blackcurrant sorbet and smiles.

"*C'est génial!*" she exclaims. It's fantastic.

It's more than just a dinner. This night is the dining equivalent of a group show in an art gallery. Everyone has a style, but together, they're highlighting a movement of their own.

In the jungle of San Francisco or Chicago restaurants, or in outposts like Houston, Peru, or Lummi Island, it can be difficult to build momentum. Here, together, they are able to show diners a cross section of the world's best cuisines.

• • •

On the other side of the kitchen doors, the dining room offers another ambience altogether. Blaine has bought little lanterns to light the deck and has had special leather menu jackets made for the occasion. Well before seven, many guests arrive for a drink on the patio, from where they can watch the chefs trot across the parking lot to the smoker and back, passing three Subarus and the swooping curves of a Rolls-Royce. On the front porch, it's about as close to a fashion show as Lummi Island ever sees, complete with designer dresses with floral patterns and plunging necklines. Despite the gravel driveway, grassy lawn, and wooden stairs, a few women teeter around on high heels.

The first guests are seated at 6:45, and the dining rooms are full by 7:15, snacks arriving in quick succession. Chef Yu sends out turnips poached in oyster juice, served in a tiny oyster shell. Chef Crenn's pink salmon with pickled-ramp mayo sits atop a homemade barley cracker that curls like a wave. Chef Achatz's green tomato gazpacho is sipped through a green onion straw crowned with tiny flowers and dill leaves. By the time the main courses begin to arrive, every diner is at full attention.

Chef Yu's raspberries are pure eye candy, with five of them arranged in a skyward-pointing cluster, bathing in the inky green of liquefied kale. The combination may be jarring in concept, but here, treating the raspberry like a vegetable and pairing it with the astringency of a few pea halves makes sense.

That plate is immediately followed by Chef Martínez's ceviche covered with tiger's milk—the latter being the bubble-gum-pink liquid he was walking around with in the kitchen, made with the fish marinade and beets. It's a surprising dish to look at—all of that bright pink covering the fish!—but it's also intensely whimsical, with its tiny, looping plant tendrils, baby flowers, and even carrot root tips rising upward. More importantly, one bite reveals it as the meal's first full-on showstopper. It is smart, light, and balanced, and it sets a high bar for everything to come.

Not to be outdone, Chef Yu's flame-roasted fingerling potatoes with dried clam sauce is a marvel of concentration of flavor, leaving some diners stomping their feet with pleasure. Every table is abuzz with people snapping photos of their dishes, a collection of little sighs and groans of pleasure, a clinking of glasses in toast after toast.

When Chef Crenn's spot prawns arrive, each is raw with the head on, but shelled and wrapped with a thin slice of venison. The scattering of wild rose petals, herb tips, tiny flowers, and little disks of turnip that surround them creates an artful presentation that Chef Crenn's artist father would likely be proud of. The mussel and foie gras mousse might appear to be a secondary element, but spooned over blackcurrant sorbet, it creates an improbable but electric combination, a true jolt that steals the limelight for a moment, but also contributes to the coherence of the dish. It also has a near-blatant sensuality, something that demands that as much of the dish as possible, particularly the prawn, be eaten with bare hands. Called "Ocean & Land" on the menu, it's a great example of a visiting chef's style and adaptability.

For his part, Blaine chooses some of his best-known dishes—fingers of salmon smoked with green alderwood, braised escarole with pickled roses, and, perhaps realizing that here as much as at any other meal, people still like warm bread, he serves his loaves with butter and chicken drippings.

Served between Chef Crenn's prawns and a Chef Achatz dish that looks like a Miró painting, it's nice to see this Willows standard toward the end of the meal.

The main courses end with Chef Kostow walking through the dining room with an entire pork collar on a large wooden cutting board, presenting the dish before slicing and plating the cut—every diner lining up for a photo. The pork, which spent much of the day in the smoker, makes its second appearance on individual plates, draped with seaweed and beach mustard. The texture is firm, the flavor from the fat leeching into the muscle. The seaweed had given up its taste of the sea but retained its snap. The play of acidity cutting the richness, the firm and pliant textures. It may have been something Kostow was trying for the first time, but it was a fully realized dish.

"I'm going to bring this one back to my restaurant," he'd say later. "We've got pork. We've got seaweed. Why not?"

Desserts arrive next. Chef Yu's deceptively simple squash blossom crème anglaise could be poured over a smoky shortbread cookie, Chef Crenn's take on Lummi Island berries looks like an edible bouquet, and, finally, Blaine's reimagining of a blueberry bush features berries so taut with juice that their skins burst with the slightest pressure.

Blaine and his crew had been preparing for weeks, burning the candle at both ends for days on end, eating most meals on their feet, making airport runs to Sea-Tac, and playing host, but now, just like that, First Harvest is over. As diners pour into the kitchen, there's finally a chance to soak in a wash of relief and excitement.

Everyone gets a round of applause, and when Blaine's turn comes, there is an even bigger cheer, led by the visiting chefs and the crew. It's met by his best aw-shucks grin. Some of the guys have a glass of wine. A bottle of Buffalo Trace appears on the pass next to the remaining slices of Chef Kostow's pork shoulder. A couple of sheet pans of cheesy nachos come out of the oven and are dusted with leftover garnish herbs and cilantro flowers.

Nobody has anything left to prove, there are no doubts about the success of the event, and everyone stands around, talking, glowing. Chef Crenn plants a big, friendly kiss on Nick's cheek, turning him beet red. Aaron's dining chart—with every square filled out with dots, slashes, and initials in ballpoint pen, highlighter, and three shades of Sharpie—looks like it's been used to plot a complex ballet.

Almost everyone retreats downhill to a bonfire on the beach. A tambourine appears, and a few people, Blaine included, jump into the chilly ocean. Some stay around the fire until dawn.

• • •

The next day, a rare Friday off at The Willows, everyone is exhausted, but recharged and ready to tear into August, the busiest month of the year.

Austin, the New York sous chef last seen running the tightest dish pass in the world, is walking on air. He's just spent two days in the kitchen helping and working with his idols.

"That," he says, "was the greatest day of my life."

# CHAPTER 5

## GOLD MINE

A text message arrives out of the blue at 10:30 on a Monday morning. The directions are vague and they involve a mountain, Smokey the Bear, an unmarked road, and the U-turn to make once you drive past the turnoff. A follow-up reads: "Bring a knife and a bag."

A week prior, there was a promise to go hunting for lobster mushrooms that never materialized, a fly-by-night page stolen directly from the truffle hunters' playbook. Gathering wild food on the island, whether it's what the cooks grab on their way in to work or something they'll make a special trip for, is never easy to schedule.

Larkin, one of Blaine's cooks, has promised Jordan, a stagiaire who's working at the Inn for the fall, that they'll go find lobster mushrooms on their day off, and they meet in the center of a large, muddy clearing in the middle of the woods at 11:00 sharp. Off to the west, a "Men's Room" sign is nailed to a large fir.

Larkin pulls his dog Isis from his car and they head north, following a whisper of a trail that alternates between easy walking and bushwhacking. The path roughly parallels Seacrest Drive, passing between tall firs and deciduous trees, and it alternates between damp and dry, depending largely on the thickness of the canopy above them. Underfoot, a carpet of pine needles, moss, and dead leaves creates a cushy layer of duff above the ground.

The trail never strays too far from Seacrest Drive, yet in the shade of the old-growth fir that's only occasionally pierced by shafts of sunlight, it feels like the heart of the forest. In the muffled quiet at ground level, 100 feet below where that canopy begins, the surroundings inspire a sense of awe. There are more than oyster mushrooms to be found. Out on the island alone, there are chanterelles, saffron milk caps, cauliflower mushrooms, and coral mushrooms.

After a week in the nonstop chaos of the kitchen, it's easy to understand why, mushrooms or no, Blaine and his cooks enjoy a walk in the woods in their free time. Even an intrepid mushroom hunter could leave this forest empty-handed and feel content.

To start their lobster mushroom hunt, they look for a low, leafy bush called salal under some fir trees, and veer off the trail when they find some, making the hiking noticeably more difficult. Jordan half-jokingly says that a machete would be useful. Isis is a muscular little mutt, and she swaps from walking to bounding, occasionally disappearing under the brush and then reappearing in a clearing to dig a hole for no particular reason.

"Okay! This is what we're looking for," Larkin says, stopping short in front of a milky-white short-stemmed russula mushroom. It is roughly the same size as a lobster mushroom, but along with having a different common name, it looks very little like what they want to find.

The russula is a good-looking, chalice-shaped mushroom with gills, but it's insipid; it won't hurt you, but it's not going to add anything to a meal. Like many mushroom varieties, russulas grow in clusters. Find some of them, and you might also find a few of their bright-orange neighbors poking up through the ground around your feet.

The explanation for the proximity between the russulas and the lobsters is funky. While the russula is still underground, an airborne fungus called *Hypomyces lactifluorum* can land on and colonize it. Much in the way airborne wild yeast can turn wort into beer, the *Hypomyces lactifluorum* effectively turns a russula into another, much tastier mushroom.

Once the fungus lands and gets to work, the gills on the russula close and the whole mushroom firms up, developing a mottled texture on top and a saturated red-orange color, a combination of factors that make it relatively easy to identify.

Despite this, picking notes have a maddening tendency to contradict themselves from one line to the next. The lobsters seem to be around moss, pines, holly, and its variants. They seem to prefer light cover—but not complete cover—overhead. At the end of the season, sometimes it's best to find some older lobsters past their prime, then look for lumps in the nearby moss and reach your hand underneath.

Here on Lummi, Isis bounds around like a small deer while Larkin roots around for a few minutes, then quietly says, "Ooh."

At his feet are a few telltale white russulas. On the ground only a few feet away are patches of the lobster's red-orange color. He picks one up, pulls a well-used, inch-wide paintbrush with short bristles from the pocket of his hoodie, and dusts off the pine needles. He flips open his pocketknife and cuts off the very bottom of the mushroom, revealing a pristine white interior. He drops it in a cloth bag and turns his eyes back to the ground. Jordan's already found another lobster, and Larkin, brushing the ground cover aside, finds more pushing up under a bed of moss. He pinches their bases to make sure they're still firm before plucking them from the ground.

The guys keep at it for the better part of two hours, going through hot spots and dead zones. They stop because they've run out of time, not for a lack of mushrooms. Between them, they've got more than twenty pounds of lobsters, with specimens ranging in size from just larger than a button mushroom to a whopper larger than a man's hand.

Take those home and sauté them in butter with shallots, garlic, and thyme and the flavor is sublime—the woodsy heart of the forest where it meets the sea. But at The Willows, Blaine has bigger ideas.

"There are so many mushrooms that we have here, and they each have their own characteristics and best ways to be cooked," he says. "Lobsters are really solid and take a lot of cooking to soften their texture. I like to cook them whole, then thinly slice them and stew the slices." Oyster mushrooms, on the other hand, are much more delicate. They will become watery and loose if sautéed, but if you poach them in a mushroom butter, they'll keep their dense texture. Delicate yellow foot chanterelles require a completely different approach.

"The yellow foot mushrooms appear in the fall with the rose hips, and they take on this great, noodle-like texture when they're lightly steamed. They're really flavorful, but you've got to stop the cooking right at the point where the aroma has just released, but before they go soft," he says. "They're also a winter mushroom, which makes them one of my favorites to collect."

To find some yellow foot mushrooms, Larkin and Jordan drive a short way down I-5, then off toward Whidbey Island on Route 20, a.k.a. Scenic Isle Way, crossing the bridge over Deception Pass. They pass horse farms dotted with grazing horses wearing thick blankets, a concrete elephant at a produce stand, and Penn Cove, home of the famous oysters of Penn Cove Shellfish. As they pull off of the highway, Isis bounces around in the back of the car. She knows they're close.

Right beneath the front bumper of the parked car are saffron milk caps beautiful enough to make Catalonians (who prize them) drool. Sitting innocuously near the trailhead is a baseball-sized *Amanita muscaria*, the hallucinogenic toadstool commonly known as the fly agaric, familiar to fans of Super Mario Bros. video games and *Alice in Wonderland*.

Today, the guys have rigged shoeboxes with a hole in one end that fit snugly inside their backpacks, allowing them to pick a mushroom and then do a sort of reverse slam dunk over their heads to put the mushroom in the box. They walk up the trail, climb a small ridge, and descend into a lush forest that dips into both micro-valleys and bowls with floors coated with pine needles.

There is an inordinate number of fallen trees, perhaps made easy to topple by the bog-like sponginess of the soil. Put your foot down near a fallen stump off trail, and you might sink up to your knee.

Time becomes elastic in the hushed space, helping to intensify the Zen-like single-mindedness of the hunt. The world and its problems melt away. Hands become thickly covered with dirt and peppered with spots of blood and tiny cuts.

A quarter mile into the woods, there's a promising and familiar sound.

"Ooh!"

Clusters of the thumb-sized fungi push out of the moss and pine needles on the forest floor. Their caps

SEA AND SMOKE

are a clay-like brown color, the gills branching off like tributaries as they move from the center to the edge. Their stems are hollow and golden brown.

These are the yellow foot and they are everywhere.

There are so many mushrooms at their feet, in fact, that the chefs start chuckling. Like fishing, mushroom hunting is inherently streaky, but on this day, they are so abundant it's like the fish are jumping into the boat.

A bit farther down the path, Jordan yells, "Gold mine!" then goes quiet for the twenty minutes it takes to fill his shoebox. There's such an abundance that the guys just end up picking as they go, stopping to admire their favorite specimens, then moving on to make a walk out of it.

Here and there, they find what they call "shy mushrooms," golden-orange hedgehogs, with their peculiar stippled gills. At one point, they think they've spotted a cluster of the prized black trumpet mushrooms, but it turns out to be a false alarm. It goes like this for an hour, wandering along the path. The scenery is calm and lush, an unassuming state park that contains a distillation of the Pacific Northwest under the cover of trees that are continuously bursting from the ground, falling over, decomposing, and growing again, forming a stand thick enough to cut out the direct light and make it almost completely diffuse. The soft ground, the tall, thin firs. An abundance hiding in plain sight.

# CHAPTER 6

## THE PERFECT SMOKE

Nick Green starts most mornings with an axe in his hand. There's a stack of wood hidden behind the smoker, and he takes a few logs over to a stump and turns cedar into kindling. This goes into the bottom of the smokehouse, a four-by-four-foot structure that's almost ten feet high, with a concrete foundation, wood sides, and a green metal roof. Nick stuffs kraft paper in the spaces between the kindling, and he sets it ablaze with a handheld BernzOmatic blowtorch. Within moments, the fire crackles ferociously, sending spark trails out the door and up into the sky.

Nick moves a few alder logs to the stump, his breath condensing in the cold November air. It's that lovely kind of wood, dried long enough to split into wedges that fly out to the sides under the weight of his axe. He moves the wedges to a flat surface and uses a well-worn hatchet to chip off the bark, and the pieces go everywhere—up onto his overcoat and into his beard and hair, where they'll likely spend the rest of the day, unnoticed.

The smoker is one of the most indispensable parts of the kitchen at The Willows, and the morning chopping is a ritual that happens every day the restaurant is open, summer or winter, rain or shine.

As he works through his morning prep, Nick tends to the fire with a pair of dedicated long-handled kitchen tongs, burning the fire down for half an hour or more, "until it looks like soot." He sets a pair of the chopped alder logs on the top, which will burn down and smolder away all day, the smoke reaching up into every crevice of the smokehouse, lacquering the walls a shiny black and gently transforming every piece of food that spends time inside.

Smokers have dotted this region for hundreds of years, an inevitable function of a region with seasonal gluts of fish and long, wet winters, but smoking food at The Willows arrived through the back door. For a time during Blaine's first year in the kitchen, longtime Lummi Islander Robert Keller swapped computer work for the Inn for the use of the kitchen's vacuum sealer, which Keller would use to seal salmon he smoked at home. "He gave me a taste of his fish one day and I was stunned," says Blaine. "If you grow up here in the Pacific Northwest, you've tasted more smoked salmon than most. But I had never smoked anything, really. I'd smoked things in the past, by torching hay in a hotel pan, but it's a different kind of flavor, and you have to be careful, or it's too much. Here on the island, I learned how delicate smoke could be."

During that first winter break, just a few months after Blaine had arrived, Willows maintenance man Theo White built a smoker just outside the kitchen doors. Now, one of the most memorable images for guests of the Inn is that of cooks trotting out to the smoker throughout the day.

Despite the "bearded lumberjack" image that it conjures, smoking at the Inn is a subtle process. Most smokers are dedicated "hot," where the smoke is near the heat source, or "cold," where the smoke is piped into an unheated space containing the food. The style favored in the Pacific Northwest uses a phone booth–shaped shed

with racks spaced out so that some are close enough to the fire to have a near-roasting effect, while others are high enough that the temperature is barely warmer than the outside air, something that varies wildly over the course of the year.

Compared to the levels of precision that can be attained in the kitchen, cooking with the smoker is something akin to taming a wild horse.

"For everything we do well in the smoker, we've tried ten other things. Like crab. Crab doesn't work. It's immediately apparent. In the beginning we worked with Robert Keller, because he really knew what he was doing. I read a lot. We advanced every day," Blaine says. "Plus, smoking fits with our style. We're out in the middle of the woods. In Seattle or in a big city, it might be a bit of a show, but here it fits with the setting."

There's more than salmon that cooks in the smoker. Throughout the day, several dishes, or components of dishes, spend time in there. Nick might open the door and find a sheet pan with cured egg yolks up and away from the heat, which will be served grated over venison tartare. Before noon, someone might trot out with a tray of shucked mussels on a bed of ice and set it—ice and all—on an upper shelf. The mussels will stay there just long enough to pick up some smoky flavor to underscore flavors in one of the first courses of the evening.

Salmon, however, is where smoking makes the most sense. More than any other dish, the two-bite portion of smoked salmon is by far the Inn's most iconic—one that displays the artistry, painstaking attention to detail, and variability that go into making a single dish work.

"It's fun to use smoke's delicate brush on meats and mushrooms, raw fish, vegetables, and even egg yolks, but we get the best salmon," Blaine says, gesturing down the road toward the reefnetters. "It's a simple thing, but I love to refine every aspect of the recipe from the fisherman to the diner."

That refinement is on display every day. Lummi Island wild sockeyes are deboned, trimmed of their collars, bellies, and tails, then cooled for a few hours to partially freeze them, making them easier to sculpt. Nick uses a long Japanese slicing knife to further trim the fillet until it is entirely uniform: a rectangle seen from above, a flattened dome looking down its length. More than a third of the fillet is trimmed away by the time he's done, but it creates a near-perfect uniformity that helps him control the smoking process.

Nick now cuts the fillet into equal ¾-inch-wide portions and places them in brine to both season the fish and firm up the flesh before drying their exteriors overnight under a fan in the fridge. During this time, the batch for tonight's dinner is pulled from the fridge, set on kraft paper, and then set in the smoker, where it will spend much of the day. If it's cold out, it takes longer. If it's warmer than normal, it comes out sooner.

Several times over the course of the day, Nick heads outside to tend the fire and test the fish for doneness. It's a process that calls as much on his successful career as an artist as his time in the kitchen at the Inn. Without that knowledge and near-constant attention, the fish will sail from perfect to overcooked in a heartbeat.

"This is a big part of the identity of the restaurant, but it's also the hardest thing I do here," he says.

While in the smoker, there's a faint sweating near the belly, and a whitish translucence forms along the arc of the cut edge. The fish is barely warm and has a firmness like the pad of a hand. A slightly tacky layer called a pellicle forms on the exterior, a reaction between the contents of the smoke and the surface of the fish. The color intensifies. The juices stay put.

"That's the way you want it to be all day long. These are the signs I'm watching for every time I go outside. I also want to make sure you're getting a smoked fish and not a baked one," says Nick. "Baked salmon gets pink, like at your mom's house. A good smoke gets redder."

These telltales, not the clock, the thermometer, or the routine, are what he uses to make sure the fish is progressing as it should be. Ask for specifics beyond those, though, and he doesn't have any. Repetition, the act of trying and experimenting again and again, has brought him to the point where he cooks completely on instinct, constantly working to hit what he calls The Perfect Smoke.

"It's much more important to pay attention to the fish than to the time or the routine."

Eventually, when he's satisfied, the fish is glazed and returned for a final hour in the smoker. It's easy to imagine even more smoke molecules sticking to the glaze. What finally emerges are portions of a color he calls "fuchsia," something that holds its shape just long enough for a diner to place it in their mouth.

For Blaine, part of the evolution of The Willows' kitchen is entrusting key tasks to other chefs. It frees him to create new dishes or tackle another part of the business, and it is a show of confidence to those who take over an important aspect of the cooking. Blaine trained Nick, and now Nick has shown a few other chefs how to do it, and by letting go, all boats are raised. Nick will eventually cede the responsibility, but even on the coldest of mornings, Blaine can still be found outside, in a quilted jacket, chopping the wood and starting the fire simply because he enjoys it.

"Working out here under the trees is a nice feeling. It's so nice," he says. "You see the ocean and the boats going by, and here I am chopping wood, and we cook this salmon, and somehow, that's my job."

# CHAPTER 7

## LAST CALL

Just before dinner service, the period during which cocktails are still going out to guests sitting on the front deck, Cameron jogs out to the grill and pushes embers around, sending orange sparks whooshing up into the twilight breeze. It's the only time during the whole day that can feel a bit relaxed. If everyone in the kitchen is ready, it can feel a little too quiet. Without everyone at their best every night, dinner would collapse in a heartbeat.

On this night, every seat is full and Aaron is expediting. He taps his pen, drumlike, next to the seating chart taped to the pass under his nose. He has to be in the groove straight out of the gate and stay there all night.

Over the course of half an hour, tables of two and four are sat, and once the first few dishes are walked out to the dining room, things start moving quickly.

"Scallops. Scallops," mutters Nick, to everyone around him and no one in particular as he floats through the kitchen as quickly as possible.

Out on the side porch where it's cooler, Blaine coaches a stagiaire through the scallop sauce: a mix of raw milk and thyme oil, making sure that each element stands out against the other, keeping the contrast of their colors as sharp as possible.

By seven, everyone is at least a drink and a course into their meal, and dinner service has ramped up to highway speed. Everyone in the kitchen has been at it for at least nine hours, and it won't even begin to slow down in here for another four.

Over on the prep bench, Cameron closes in on the last of the roe rolls, and the inside edge of the sheet pan he's using as a workspace has a neat line of dabs of cream that come from squaring off each end of the tube. When the last one goes out to the dining room, he slides the tray under the lip of the bench with one hand and whips the towel off of his waist with the other. In one motion, he clears the bench with the towel, sweeping any stray crumbs into the tray, and disappears with it toward the dishwasher.

The grid on the sheet under Aaron's nose fills with dots, dashes, and scribbles, the house system that involves pens and Sharpies in several colors, and spells out everything from if a table has been cleared, to if the wine has been poured, to the initials of the person who served each dish. Taking up much of the sheet is the party of ten in the private dining room, a crew from Seattle's top-shelf Canlis restaurant. They're here to eat, see what their friends at The Willows are up to, watch the kitchen run, and drink a lot of great wine in the process.

On a busy night like this one, their table of ten can be a backbreaker for a kitchen to work around: getting ten dishes ready at once is a huge feat that can cause a major disruption in the service to all of the smaller tables of two and four, and it happens every course, all night long.

In the back, Cameron the dishwasher moves fast in the dish pit. He's all lateral motion, sliding back and forth like a tennis player hitting shots from the baseline. Up front, Aaron hustles in place. "Three and six are next. Three and

six," he says to himself, rattling off table numbers, then looking up at the chefs around him, he says, "A beet and a scallop, then two scallops. The beet is the first thing. Beet, Nick, that's your boy."

Right here, Blaine reminds a cook to make sure that he is in step with the staff when he brings a dish to a table, something that allows the staff to walk around a table, then away from it, without bumping into each other. It's a public admonition but delivered gently enough to remind everyone to be on their toes. Moments later, Blaine sends that same cook back out to serve again: a vote of confidence and an assurance that everything is okay.

As this happens, an enthusiastic, jovial diner appears in the kitchen, announces his approval of the meal as a whole, and disappears back onto the floor. It's a little indication of the mood of ease and contentment—often bordering on bliss—that the front-of-house team works to curate just ten feet away from the kitchen. Every night, while the kitchen churns away, Blaine's partner and girlfriend, Raquel, runs the floor.

The basics and the grind—the capable ferrying of plates, the thorough understanding of the menu, the service with a smile, and the capacity to do it all under pressure? Those are the skills each front-of-house staff member needs to have nailed a couple years before dropping off a résumé at The Willows. What Raquel's really after are people who can do all that and also maintain the ambience that helps everyone sitting in the dining room to have the best night of their lives.

"Every night is different. You get to know different people every service, and there's drama all over the place," she says, noting the Inn's stellar marriage-proposal-acceptance record. "We have to get here and make sure that all of our personal drama stays at home.

Everybody's got to come together, regroup, and be in the right mindset."

When the weather's nice, that mood starts out on the deck before dinner, where smiling visitors tend to do a lot of picture taking and one or two couples are invariably flipping through a food magazine. The waitstaff glides through with small trays, their drinks glinting in the sunlight. There's a seamless grace reminiscent of the way a performance artist makes their work seem effortless. Emily, who is in charge of the bar, might drop off drinks at a table, then—in the time it takes to turn around—she'll scan six other tables to make sure they're doing well while tucking in a chair. If one member of a couple gets up to powder her nose, a server is there a beat later, folding her napkin and talking to the customer at the table.

Raquel is a natural at straddling the line between the kitchen and the customers, moving back and forth between the energy and concentration of the kitchen and the jovial mood on the floor.

"My original plan was to work in a kitchen. I went to culinary school, but I wanted more contact with people, to be able to talk to them and make them feel cared for," she says.

After culinary school, she spent four years cutting her teeth working through the different stations at a couple of restaurants in Las Vegas and Seattle, but she found her groove as she worked her way up through the ranks on the service side at L'Auberge Carmel in California. She worked as an expediter, server, and then assistant manager, learning the finer points of service from their master sommelier and the owner.

"I love watching the customers' eyes and faces. I love answering their questions and bringing them into the kitchen."

When the manager left, she was a shoo-in. It also left her in a perfect position to run the floor at The Willows.

"Here, you get to know new people and see old friends every night. You have to love every table and who they are. Every interaction has to be sincere."

Or what?

"It doesn't work. You can see a fake smile a mile away. We want people to feel like they're among old friends while they're here. Every night is like a little movie, and when you're living it, you know you're doing it well."

Back in the kitchen, mushrooms with juniper purée, the dishes painted bright green with the purée and showcasing the diversity of mushroom season in full flush, are being sent out. A few dishes before the end, the cooks realize they're a few matsutakes shy. They look at each other without saying a word and then at the tray full of whole mushrooms that had just been walked through the dining room and shown to the diners. Aaron grabs two of those matsutakes, essentially grabbing garments off a mannequin, and uses the mandoline to shave them over top of the remaining dishes. Problem solved.

Back at the flattop, Nick is a modern-day saucier. At any given time he has ten to twenty pots and pans on the heat, many of them labeled with a paper tag and all within an arm's reach. Stuff that needs blazing heat is kept in the back-left corner, and pots at the cooler front-right corner have their bottom edges tipped into the "moat" surrounding the flattop, essentially parked while being kept nearby. Above Nick's head, a stack of wrapped sheet pans and a dozen saucepans, all loaded with components of dishes to come later in the evening, is ready to roll. At his knees below the temperature-control knobs is a lowboy: drawers and cold storage where prep kits, including things like dish garnishes, sauces, and horseradish that will be integrated into a crab and seaweed dish, are kept cool until the last minute.

Twenty minutes before the first duck and turnip dish is served, Nick clears a space in the center of the grill, scrapes it clean with a pastry knife, and sets five aged duck breasts in the center of the grill, skin-sides down, the duck plumping almost as soon as it hits the heat.

Once it crisps, Nick next drops handfuls of butter cubes on the cooler end of the grill, flipping the breasts and setting the meat directly on the rapidly melting blocks. This slows the cooking and keeps the meat from seizing too much, while the steam from the water in the butter helps it to cook evenly. Working quickly, he tips the breasts on their sides like fallen dominoes, tucking more cubes of butter into the spaces between each one, then flips them on their opposite edges, gently cooking their outside surfaces.

Nick taps each one to check for doneness, remembering to run a pastry knife across the top of the grill to keep the smoke down, followed by a cloth around its outside edge, nice and neat. When they're done, the breasts are set on a rack to rest for four minutes before serving. Keeping them skin-side down, the skin stays crisp and the flesh remains pink and moist.

After resting, they're a perfect pink, all the way through. The fat in the skin on the top is almost completely rendered, amazingly flat (thanks to some artful trimming while it was being butchered), and ready to be dusted with fleur de sel.

When those go out to the dining room, it marks the last big push of the night, when dishes in varying states of readiness almost completely cover the pass.

Outside, it's dark enough that the first things you notice are the sound of the sea, the blink of a buoy miles out toward the horizon, and the silhouette of the pines backlit by stars, but inside, the dining room is loud. The gestures are large, the smiles wide. The last duck dish heads out of the kitchen, and the focus immediately turns to dessert. Nothing becomes less important, nobody slows down, but the light at the end of the tunnel has come into view. Blaine and Aaron take advantage of the pre-dessert lull to scrub, squeegee, and towel-dry the pass and prep bench.

Once the last dessert is out and the kitchen has been scoured for the last time, the cooks hang around for just a bit before heading home; prep for tomorrow's service starts early the next morning.

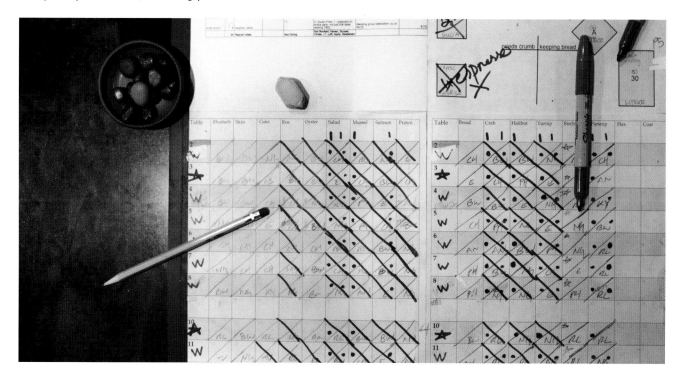

# HOW TO USE THIS BOOK

## BY BLAINE WETZEL

Coming to Lummi Island was a pleasantly overwhelming experience. I had one notion of what cooking should be, but arriving here revised my ideas about food and how I wanted to share it with others. This book is an attempt to show you my processes and how this rich island changed my perspective.

Moving from a metropolitan city center in Europe to a small, remote island, I knew my surroundings would be different, but what I didn't think about as much was the way my connection to food and ingredients would be altered. An apple on Lummi Island is very unlike an apple in Seattle, New York, or Copenhagen. Many ingredients I was so familiar with ended up tasting different here, almost as if I were tasting them for the first time. I love centering our food around a natural ingredient's amazing flavor and sharing something so undeniably good with a guest. That idea alone motivates me to cook.

Our creations have life cycles. Some dishes are perennial favorites, and we look forward to putting them on the menu for a short time each year; others evolve from year to year. They emerge, they go away to hibernate, and they resurface as something different. There are ingredients that come into our kitchen with such an extremely short season that we'll create a simple way to highlight the ingredient to make sure it's included on the menu in time. Other products give us the flexibility to spend great amounts of time working with them to master the perfect recipe. A great dinner menu contains both kinds of dishes. Our challenge here is to capture that fleeting moment, when something has

the perfect taste and texture, and we try to do that with a menu's worth of different ingredients and different dishes every night.

Joe Ray spent a year living on the island and working his ass off in the kitchen and at the farm, and he did an extremely thorough job of recording and converting our recipes from the 2013 to 2014 season. Here in the kitchen, our "recipes" tend to be a few lines scribbled in a notebook, listed quantities and almost no procedures. In fact, for a while Joe had the only complete copy of most of what we did. Unlike the first seven chapters of the book, which were written by Joe, the voice in the headnotes is mine: it was important to me to explain our process, from ingredients to finished dish, in my own words.

The recipes in this book represent a moment in time, the product of an amazing year, and they came together through experimentation and our access to amazing ingredients. Part of Joe's work was to capture those moments on paper, and if you have access to fantastic ingredients, these recipes will get you as close as possible to what we made.

Just as important, I hope that they will inspire you to make your own creations. Use your intuition and these recipes to guide you to make your own food taste great. Remember to taste at every step—tasting is almost never emphasized enough.

These recipes are written according to how we cook them in the kitchen at The Willows and are based on the cooking times and temperatures specific to

our hearth oven, stove, smokehouse, and grill. They'll certainly be different from those in your kitchen, so pay close attention and use your own judgment to guide cooking times and doneness. Similarly, these recipes are measured with our ingredients and might vary significantly from what you use. Spend the extra time to source all of your ingredients carefully. Many of the recipes are so straightforward that without exceptional ingredients they are not worth attempting.

Sometimes it is tough to completely scale down a recipe to produce only four portions, so we give the smallest reasonable portions for such recipes.

We've strived to give measurements in both metric and U.S. systems, and if appropriate, we just call for a spoonful of something. That said, metric is what we use in the kitchen and what will always provide the most consistent results. We call for prepping garnish ingredients first, as it eliminates needing to prep them just before serving a dish. Keep them in a container lined with paper towels in the refrigerator.

The basis for most of these recipes is incredible ingredients that speak to you. You might find a few unusual things listed in these pages, but they're not exotic in that they're expensive and rare, just hyperlocal.

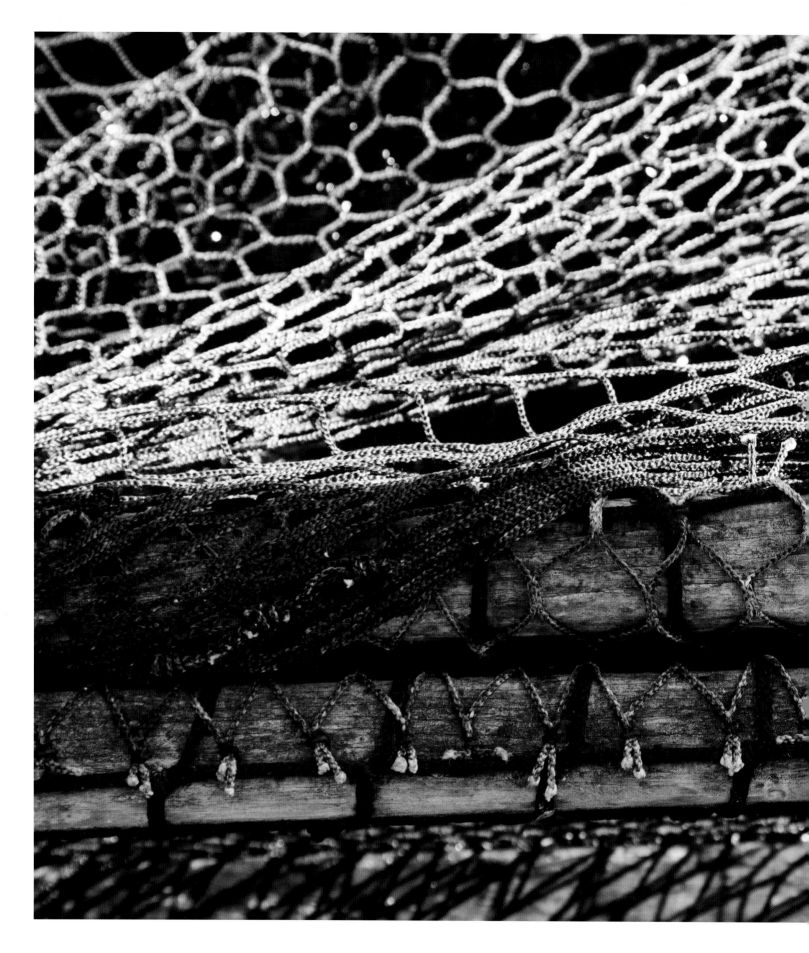

# RECIPES

# CAVIAR AND CRÊPES

We are lucky to buy whole salmon direct from our reefnet fishermen. The fish go straight from their boat to a skiff and then over to The Willows, often for less than a dollar a pound. We buy as many fish as we need for a year's worth of roe in a four-week period. On these first few days, the roe has a creamy texture like a chicken egg yolk, and we like to serve a slice of barely seared roe sack with a sprinkle of sea salt over the top.

The reefnet boats are a stone's throw offshore. When they fish in the summer, they can catch thousands of salmon each day, and usually one of the fishermen's wives will sit on the roadside by the boats, selling just-caught salmon from a cooler.

Once a salmon is caught, the quality of its roe deteriorates by the hour. The eggs are held together in a membrane, and all of these connections and any blood vessels must be removed quickly and entirely before the eggs can be cured and stored.

When the salmon starts coming into the kitchen, we are processing fish and curing roe nonstop, fifty fish at a time, every other day. It's a painstaking process, but any chef who has worked at The Willows for a reasonable amount of time will most likely become very good at butchering fish.

SERVES 4

## FOR THE ROLLS

2 (12-inch/30 cm) thin crêpes (brik dough)

2 fresh egg whites, preferably from Riley Starks, lightly beaten

2 tablespoons/30 g clarified high-quality unsalted butter

## FOR THE MAPLE-SHERRY CREAM

¼ cup/60 g heavy whipping cream

¾ teaspoon/4.5 g barrel-aged sherry vinegar

¾ teaspoon/6 g bigleaf maple syrup

## FOR SERVING

2 ounces/55 g cured salmon roe (page 254)

¼ cup/10 g finely chopped chives (about 1⁄16 inch/2 mm)

## ROLLS

Cut the crêpes into 16 (3½ x 1½-inch/9 x 4 cm) strips, immediately covering them with a damp cloth to keep them from drying out. You'll use 8 strips but this will make several extra, as they're prone to breaking.

Paint a thick coat of egg white, about 14 x 10 inches/35 x 25 cm, onto a cutting board. Neatly lay the strips of crêpe, side by side, onto it, lining the ends up precisely and leaving a finger's width of space between each. Brush the upward-facing surface of the crêpe strips with more egg white.

Brush two 12-inch/30 cm cannoli molds with some of the clarified butter and lay them across the centerline of the pastry strips. Wrap the strips neatly around the molds—a small offset spatula works well here—maintaining the space between each strip and not drawing them too tightly around the pipes. The ends of each strip should just overlap.

Heat a convection oven to 365°F/185°C. Line a half-sheet pan with a Silpat mat or parchment paper and brush the surface with the remaining clarified butter. Gently lay in the cannoli molds, placing the overlapping ends of the crêpe strips down on the pan. Use small, clean rocks (or other weights) at the ends of the molds to keep them separated on the tray and to prevent them from rolling.

Bake until the rolls are crisp and golden brown, about 25 minutes. When the molds are cool enough to touch, gently ease the rolls off, one at a time. There will likely be a fair amount of breakage, particularly the first few times you try this. Store the completely cooled rolls, close-packed and standing vertically, in a parchment-lined airtight storage container until serving.

## MAPLE-SHERRY CREAM

Whisk the heavy cream in a 12-inch/30 cm metal mixing bowl until it thickens (traces will appear in the cream behind the whisk, but no peaks). Add the sherry vinegar and the maple syrup to the cream and whisk until soft-to-medium peaks form, then transfer the cream into a plastic piping bag fitted with a pastry tip small enough to fit into the rolls. Keep cool until ready to serve.

## TO SERVE

To serve, set 8 empty rolls vertically on a small sheet pan lined with parchment paper. Fill the bottom third of each roll with cream, use a spoon to fill the middle third with the roe, and fill the top third with cream. Lift the rolls out one at a time and use a flat spatula to create nice, flat ends. Dip each end in the chives and place the rolls on a small serving plate, ends out.

# SMOKED MUSSELS

When I first started at The Willows, Chef Sam Nutter came to the island to help me out for the first month or so. Sam's a good friend, and he and Raquel and I would head out in a rowboat to collect mussels that clung to the underside of nearby buoys. A good haul might yield 40 pounds of mussels from the bottom of each one.

As the restaurant grew, I started looking for a local source for mussels. We are lucky to be just around the corner from several shellfish farms. My favorite, Taylor Shellfish Farms in Samish Bay, produces many types of incredible clams, mussels, oysters, and even scallops. It is worth the short trip south, which we make every other day.

Mussel flavor and quality changes quickly, and using just-harvested mussels is essential when smoking them, otherwise their flavor gets too strong. For this dish, I smoke the mussels lightly, keeping them cold as the smoke washes over them for about four hours. This gentle smoking creates a complex flavor, without any bitterness.

Once smoked, I sear them on high heat, allowing the natural sugars and amino acids to form a crisp, dark crust on both sides. They have to be cooked fairly thoroughly in order to taste good; raw or partially raw is not good in this preparation. That said, it's important to serve this straight away after cooking. A thoroughly cooked mussel does not stay juicy and delicious for very long.

We serve the mussel in its shell in a cedar box that billows alderwood smoke when opened.

YIELDS 10 MUSSELS

10 Samish Bay mussels (about 300 g)
1 cup/240 g mussel stock (page 246)
Grapeseed oil
Few teaspoons finely ground alderwood chips

Prepare a smoker (a cold smoker is preferable) and set a perforated pan full of ice over a hotel pan.

Rinse the mussels quickly under cold water, leaving the beard attached. Bring the mussel stock to a boil in a medium saucepan, add the mussels, cover, and cook until they're just starting to open, about 15 to 30 seconds, then immediately place them on a tray on top of the bed of ice. (If you're making a larger amount of mussels, do this step in batches to allow the mussels to cook in a single layer in the bottom of the pot.)

Once they're cool enough to handle, gently pull the mussels out of their shells (a small offset spatula is nice for this), trim the beard off the shells with scissors, and place the mussels on a double layer of paper towels on a quarter-sheet pan, reserving the shells for serving.

Set the mussels, still on their sheet pan, on top of the ice and place the pans and ice into the smoker. Smoke the mussels away from the heat for 4 to 5 hours, replenishing the ice, if necessary—they're ready when a seared mussel (see below) has a nice balance between sweet and smoky.

While the mussels smoke, gently scrub their shells clean and keep them covered with a damp paper towel until serving.

To serve, warm the mussel shells in the oven at 300°F/150°C.

Pour a thin layer of grapeseed oil in a skillet set over high heat and sear both sides of the mussels until deeply caramelized. Return the mussels to their shells and put each one in a serving box. Pipe a puff of alderwood smoke into each box with a handheld food smoker, replace the lid, and serve immediately.

# HERRING ROE ON KELP WITH CHARRED DANDELIONS

In 2011, when I was getting to know my new home on Lummi, I researched the food traditions of the coastal First Peoples who inhabited the region centuries ago. One of the foods that I was most interested in was the kelp leaves that become covered in sticky herring roe when the fish spawn, which the First Peoples dried. The more I found out, the more eagerly I awaited the coming season and the opportunity to try to find and cook with them.

No one knows exactly when the herring will spawn, but it is close to the same time each year, so we guessed. We closed the restaurant for three days while the whole kitchen staff traveled all the way up to the waters off of Sitka, Alaska, in search of herring roe on kelp.

We guessed right and were greeted with cloudy-green waters and glistening beaches covered in roe. The herring spawned in such large numbers that their eggs left an inch-thick coating on all the seaweed we found. We packed it in salt and headed home with as much as we could possibly carry.

We've made the trip to Alaska several times since then and served the roe in several ways. Simply sautéing some leaves of roe-covered seaweed in whole butter makes a delicious serving, but in this recipe, we soak the seaweed and roe in several changes of water to leach out some of the salt, then sear whole sections on the plancha in clarified butter before dehydrating and grating them over spring dandelion leaves.

Dandelion? The weed? While cultivated dandelions are becoming a familiar ingredient on menus, we prefer their wild cousins.

If diners suspect that we've pulled the dandelions from a nearby yard and are charging a lot of money for weeds, they're often correct. The irony is that this dish is one of the most labor-intensive on the menu. The flavor wins over any skeptics. We use early spring dandelions for this dish, which means they're a bit more tender but still quite bitter. Grilling mellows some of their bitterness, and we balance that out by grating the dried seaweed and roe over the top along with a drizzle of rendered lardo.

SERVES 4

4 ounces/100 g brined herring roe on kelp

5 ounces/150 g trimmed high-quality lardo

30 young dandelion plants (picked before flowering)
  with 3-inch/8 cm leaves, taproot attached

2 tablespoons/25 g grapeseed oil

Verjus

Flake salt

4 skinned, blanched hazelnuts

### DRIED HERRING ROE

Soak the herring roe on kelp in cold, fresh water for at least 40 minutes, changing the water every 10 minutes. Slice and pan-fry a small piece of the roe to test for seasoning; it will be very salty but palatable when ready. Sear the roe-covered leaves in a little grapeseed oil until golden.

Dry the roe overnight in a single layer in a dehydrator set to high until completely dry. Reserve in an airtight container.

### RENDERED LARDO

Rough chop the lardo into cubes and set them in a small pot over medium-low heat until the fat is fully rendered (any remaining solid pieces will be crisp), about 1 hour. Strain out and discard the solids and keep the rendered lardo warm.

### GRILLED DANDELIONS

Prepare a fire for direct grilling. Halve any dandelion plants that are wider than ½ inch/1 cm at the base. In a mixing bowl, coat the dandelions with the grapeseed oil and a splash of verjus. Grill the dandelions until the bases are tender and the leaves are charred, about 2 minutes. In a mixing bowl, dress the dandelions with about 2 tablespoons of hot lardo and salt sparingly.

### TO SERVE

Arrange about 5 dandelions across each warmed dinner plate. Add a small drizzle of hot lardo to each dandelion base. Using a Microplane, grate a blanched hazelnut over the dandelions on each plate, followed by an equal amount of grated roe.

# SCALLOPS FROM FANNY BAY

At the height of winter, the live scallops that we buy arrive at the restaurant literally clapping their shells. We keep them alive until the moment before they are served, when we gently remove the top shell, clean away the skirts and any organs, and scrape out portions from the still-quivering adductor muscle using the top shell.

Just-harvested raw scallops have a very clean flavor, and we use very fresh milk to accentuate their creamy sweetness.

SERVES 4

4 live Fanny Bay scallops (about 1 pound 3 ounces/1 kg)
¼ cup/60 g very fresh whole milk
Dill oil (page 242)
1-inch/2.5 cm piece fresh horseradish root (about 35 g)
Flake salt
4 teaspoons/5 g finely chopped dill stems

Gently take off the top shell of the scallops using a palette knife. Remove the skirts, roe, and any viscera.

Use the top shell to scrape the adductor muscle into small pieces (like a tartare), adding the milk as you go. (This dish is served in the lower half of the shell.) Drizzle a few drops of dill oil over the scallop, followed by a grating of horseradish, a sprinkle of salt, and a teaspoon/1.25 g of dill stems.

# A STEW OF STINGING NETTLES

Nettles are the very first of many plants that we collect around the island at the outset of spring. They poke up from damp, recently roughed-up soil while the rest of the forest still seems to be completely dormant, and lucky for us, their appearance tends to coincide with The Willows' reopening in early spring. We serve them with a few of the other wild edibles that pop up and quickly vanish at the end of the winter, like pine shoots and salmonberry blossoms, giving the dish a clear sense of time and place, and giving us a sense of relief from the dreary feelings that sometimes creep up during the Pacific Northwest's dark and drizzly winters.

The flavor of nettles is full of a wild greenness that is difficult to capture when cooked. This is made even trickier by the long cooking time needed to soften them into palatability. To compensate, we combine a few different nettle preparations in what appears to be a simple dish in order to capture the great aroma of fresh, raw nettles in a cooked dish. I like to serve this taste of early spring with a slice of just-set raw cow's milk cheese because the textures work so well together.

SERVES 4

**FOR THE GARNISH**

20 spruce tips

20 salmonberry shoots

12 salmonberry blossoms

**FOR THE NETTLES**

1 bunch stinging nettles (about 1 pound/450 g)

42 ounces/1.25 L light vegetable stock (page 250)

2 tablespoons/30 g high-quality unsalted butter, divided

½ cup/5 g parsley leaves

Flake salt

3¾ ounces/105 g baby spinach, stems trimmed

1 tablespoon/15 g reduced white wine (page 251)

3½ tablespoons/50 g spinach purée (page 247), divided

High-quality cider vinegar

¼ cup/45 g fresh cheese (page 251)

Wearing kitchen gloves, separate the nettles into three containers: the tender leaves at the top with the stems removed in one, the more mature leaves in another, and the stems, roughly chopped, in the third.

## NETTLE SAUCE

Bring the light vegetable stock to a simmer, then pour it over about a quarter of the roughly chopped stems in a pot or metal bowl. Allow the mixture to steep until the stock takes on a pronounced nettle flavor, about 2 minutes, then strain out and discard the stems.

Pour 1 cup/250 ml of the still-hot stock into a 1-quart/1 L container. Add about a third of the mature nettle leaves and push them down into the stock so that they wilt. (The rest of the mature leaves will not be used.) Place the stock and wilted nettle leaves in the blender and blend, starting on low speed and working up to high, until the mixture is liquid with only tiny particles of the nettle leaves. Pour the liquid into a metal container in an ice bath and let completely cool.

Pour the cooled liquid over the remaining roughly chopped stems and steep for 2 minutes. Strain the liquid through a Superbag and discard the solids.

## STEWED NETTLE LEAVES

Place a medium saucepan over medium heat and add 1½ tablespoons/22 g of the butter, along with the parsley leaves and the tender nettle leaves, stirring frequently. After a few minutes, add ¼ cup/60 g of the puréed nettle sauce, cook it down until it has a stew-like consistency, then add another ¼ cup/60 g of the sauce and cook that down, too. The leaves will be tender but will retain their vibrant green color. Add a large pinch of salt, continue to stir for about 2 minutes, then stir in the baby spinach and cook until the vegetables take on an almost silky texture, about 2 more minutes.

Add the reduced white wine, 1½ tablespoons/22 g of the spinach purée, and salt to taste, then stir in the remaining spinach purée and the remaining butter. The leaves will take on a deep, glowing green. Season with a few drops of cider vinegar.

In a small saucepan, warm ½ cup/120 g of the nettle sauce over low heat.

## TO SERVE

Place a large spoonful of stewed nettles at the center of a plate, flattening them with the back of a spoon to create a disk about 3 inches/7.5 cm across. Spread a tablespoon of the warm nettle sauce over the top of the disk.

Set a bite-sized spoonful of fresh cheese on top of the stewed nettles and garnish with the spruce tips and the salmonberry shoots and blossoms.

# HALIBUT SKINS WRAPPED AROUND CLAMS
## AND **ROLLED IN SEAWEED**

love fish skin crisped over the grill, but a nice, soggy fish skin, with its velvety texture, collagen, and fat, is one of my favorite things to eat. We first started serving this dish at the restaurant to make use of the skins from the fish we served, but soon we had to ask the fishermen we knew for their halibut skins as well. Those were mostly going into the garbage anyway, so we were able to get the main ingredient for one of our most popular snacks out of something that is often discarded, which is always a good feeling.

SERVES 4

**FOR THE POWDERED SEAWEED**

1 pound/500 g fresh ulva seaweed

½ ounce/15 g tapioca maltodextrin

**FOR THE HALIBUT SKIN**

Skin from a 5-pound/2.25 kg halibut fillet, scraped clean

Olive oil

Grapeseed oil

**FOR THE FARCE**

35 medium Samish Bay clams (about 1 kg)

½ cup/120 g dry white wine

1 tablespoon/10 g chopped shallots

2 tablespoons/30 g verjus

3½ ounces/100 g raw halibut, diced and frozen

7 tablespoons/100 g cold clam stock (page 246)

10 tablespoons/150 g cold grapeseed oil

2 teaspoons/10 g salt

## POWDERED SEAWEED

Dehydrate the seaweed overnight at 100°F/38°C. It should be crisp when finished.

Put the seaweed in the blender with the tapioca maltodextrin and blend it on medium until a powder is formed.

## HALIBUT SKIN

Half fill a medium saucepan with water and bring it to a boil. Add the halibut skin and simmer for 24 minutes. Coat a Silpat mat with enough olive oil to set the skin on, lay the skin on top, and place the mat in front of a fan overnight.

Heat a fryer with grapeseed oil to 350°F/175°C. Cut the halibut skin into 4 pieces, each roughly 3 x 3 inches/7.5 x 7.5 cm. Flash fry the skins until they are crisp and have doubled in thickness, about 20 seconds, and set them on a paper towel–lined tray. Working quickly, use a set of long kitchen tweezers to roll the halibut skins into a cone shape.

## FARCE

Steam the clams with the wine in a medium saucepan over medium-high heat until the clams just start to open. Set the clams on a bed of ice for 5 minutes, then pull them out of their shells. Remove their stomachs with a pair of scissors and discard.

Bring the shallots and verjus to a boil over high heat and pour them into a blender with the frozen halibut cubes and cold clam stock. Blend on medium until incorporated, then add the cold grapeseed oil slowly (as with a mayonnaise), followed by the salt. Pass the mixture through a fine-mesh sieve, fold in the clams, and transfer the mixture to a piping bag.

## TO SERVE

Roll the crisp halibut skins in the seaweed powder, and pipe the farce into each cone.

# NOOTKA ROSE PETALS AND SALMONBERRIES

Salmonberries and Nootka roses grow along the beaches and in the woods around the island, enjoying similar habitats and often intertwining with each other. There are about two weeks a year when the berries are ripe and the roses are in bloom, and if all goes well, I can pick some of both on my way to work. Enough roses for a week can sometimes be had for just a half hour's work, while a similar effort gives you just an evening's worth of berries.

Rose hips, the fruit from the rose bushes, is the sleeper ingredient in this recipe and something that makes each bite of the granita taste like a fistful of fresh roses. After the first frost each year, we collect the rose hips and use them in a few ways, one of which is in this highly flavorful oil made from blending a large amount of the rose hips with a small amount of neutral oil and allowing it to infuse for a few days. The combination of the fresh granita, the rose hip oil, and the wild salmonberries makes for one of my favorite dishes of the year.

SERVES 4

### FOR THE ROSE GRANITA

1 pint gently packed Nootka rose petals (about 18 g)

1 cup/265 g Stock syrup (page 256), divided

½ cup/120 g verjus

### FOR THE SALMONBERRY JUICE

6 ounces/170 g salmonberries

Stock syrup (page 256)

Verjus

32 perfect salmonberries

### FOR SERVING

64 Nootka rose petals

Dried rose hip–infused oil

## ROSE GRANITA

Combine the pint/18 g of rose petals, half of the stock syrup, and a tablespoon/15 g of water in a blender and blend on high until a rough purée forms. Vacuum seal the purée in a sous vide bag and refrigerate it overnight. Pass the purée through a Superbag and dilute it with about 1 cup/235 g of water—you want to bring it to a palatable level of bitterness—then season it with the remaining stock syrup and the verjus. (It's important to taste as you add the water, syrup, and verjus here, as you're working backward from a concentrated flavor to an enjoyable one.)

Pour the mixture into a shallow container that will give it about 1 inch/2.5 cm of depth, cover, and freeze until it becomes slushy, then carefully mix it with an immersion blender. Cover the container and return it to the freezer until the mixture is frozen solid. No more than a few hours before you're planning on serving, scrape the frozen mix in a crosshatch pattern with a sturdy fork until reduced to a granita texture, then cover and return it to the freezer.

## SALMONBERRY JUICE

Put the 6 ounces/170 g of salmonberries in a blender and blend on high until they are liquefied. Strain the juice through a Superbag and refrigerate it for an hour. Gently pour it into a separate container, leaving any particles that have settled at the bottom of the first container. Season the juice with stock syrup and verjus. Place serving bowls in the freezer to chill.

## TO SERVE

Arrange 8 salmonberries together in a circle at the bottom of each chilled serving bowl. Spoon in a tablespoon of salmonberry juice and arrange 16 rose petals on top of and up against the berries. Give the granita a good stir, then gently sprinkle about 2 tablespoons of it over the berries, drizzle with rose hip–infused oil, and serve immediately.

# STEAMED RHUBARB
## WITH **SPRUCE BRANCHES** AND **ANGELICA LEAVES**

Rhubarb is a harbinger of spring in the Pacific Northwest. It's hard not to get excited about the refreshing and surprisingly fruit-like flavor that rhubarb brings to our plates as early as March, when real fruit is still a couple of months away. This method of cooking the rhubarb really brings out its fruitiness, both in flavor and texture.

This dessert tries to home in on the amazing affinity that rhubarb, pine, and angelica have for one another. Many people wouldn't consider pine a culinary ingredient. The older needles are bitter and resinous, but the young shoots from mid-spring are tender and brightly flavored, with a mild and pleasing astringency. The overall effect is something like lemon zest, making anything it's served with taste bright and fresh. I like to finish the dish with a whipped cream infused with the wonderfully clean, green flavors of very young angelica.

SERVES 4

4 ounces/100 g angelica leaves

½ cup/125 g high-quality heavy cream

6 stalks 1 inch-/2.5 cm-thick rhubarb (about 375 g), divided

2 tablespoons/30 g 20% stock syrup (made by decreasing the proportion of sugar in the standard stock syrup recipe, page 256)

1 tablespoon/13 g granulated sugar, plus more to taste

24 pine tips

4 teaspoons/10 g bay leaf crumble (page 216)

Juniper oil (page 242)

Thyme oil (page 242)

## ANGELICA CREAM

Pack the angelica leaves into the bottom of a 1-quart/1 L container, pour the heavy cream over the top, cover, and allow to steep overnight in the refrigerator. Strain the cream through a Superbag into a metal mixing bowl and reserve it in the refrigerator until serving.

## RHUBARB STALKS

Preheat a sous vide water bath to 140°F/60°C. Clean and cut 12 sections of rhubarb stalks that are 3 inches/7.5 cm long. Place the sections in a sous vide bag in a single layer. Add the stock syrup to the bag and vacuum seal on medium.

Place the bag in the water bath until the stalks begin to give way under thumb pressure, 8 to 12 minutes, then cool in an ice bath. Remove the stalks from the bag and set them on a parchment-lined half-sheet pan and reserve in the refrigerator. Reserve the syrup in a sealed container to season the rhubarb juice and cubes in the next steps.

## RHUBARB JUICE

Run enough remaining raw stalks of rhubarb through a juicer to make about ¼ cup/60 g of rhubarb juice; season with some of the syrup from the cooked stalks.

## RHUBARB CUBES

Create 24 ¼-inch/.5 cm cubes from the remaining raw rhubarb. Place the cubes in a sous vide bag with the remaining reserved syrup and run them through the vacuum sealer on high.

## TO SERVE

Add the sugar to the angelica cream and whip it until very soft peaks form, tasting to see if more sugar is needed once the granules have dissolved.

Place 2 cooked rhubarb stalks side by side in each dessert bowl. Arrange 8 rhubarb cubes on top of them and garnish with 6 pine tips. Place a teaspoon/2.5 g of bay leaf crumble off to one side and a dollop of the whipped cream on top of it. Spoon 2 teaspoons of rhubarb juice into the bowl, then add a few drops of the juniper and thyme oils on top of the rhubarb juice.

# A BROTH OF ROASTED MADRONA BARK

Madronas are beautiful trees with bark that peels off in red curls, revealing a smooth, lacquer-like flesh of whites and greens near the trunk. Varicolored branches with peeling bark hang over the rockier shores of the southern end of the island. Walking through the madronas during the early fall as the trees shed their bark is a stunning sight.

We collect the bark as it falls from the trees and also prune the small branches, roast them, and steep them in water to make a broth that is a natural digestive and lovely to drink after a main course of rich lamb or deer.

YIELDS A BIT LESS THAN 2 QUARTS/2 L

1¼ pounds/600 g madrona branches, broken into 6-inch/15 cm lengths

Stock syrup (page 256)

4 ounces/110 g madrona bark, torn into 1-inch/2.5 cm pieces

Preheat the oven to 465°F/240°C. Place the branches in a roasting pan and toast them in the oven until they begin to darken and become fragrant, 10 to 15 minutes.

Transfer the branches to a large stockpot filled with 2 quarts/2 L of water. Cover with parchment paper cut to fit directly on the water's surface, followed by a flat, clean rock on top of the parchment to keep the branches submerged. Set the pot over low heat and allow it to steep until tinted like tea, about an hour, then strain with a fine-mesh sieve. Season the broth with just enough stock syrup to cut the bitterness.

## TO SERVE

Pour the hot broth into a bowl with the madrona bark pieces and let it steep for 2 minutes, then strain the broth into teacups.

# AGED VENISON AND WILD LETTUCE WITH SEEDED BREAD

Isaac is a Lummi Islander who used to be a dishwasher at the restaurant. He's also a bowhunter, and one morning, he brought in a still-warm deer heart wrapped in pages torn from a *Playboy* magazine. He handed it to me, pointing out the nick in the heart from the arrow, showing off what a good shot he was.

We sliced it thin, sprinkled a little salt over the top, and ate it right there in the kitchen as a display of manliness and to promote facial-hair growth.

It is amazing how different wild animals taste. They run and fight and fuck and starve. They eat leaves and twigs and berries. You can taste it all in their flavor and texture, something so glaring that it's hard to consider them the same species as their domesticated counterparts.

For the tartare in this recipe, it's important to use a tough muscle from wild venison that's been aged for a long time. I like to use a shoulder hung for at least six weeks. The meat must be thoroughly cleaned of connective tissue (the spot where any perceived toughness lies) before being diced. It should be served ice cold with hot slices of toasted rye bread and some just-picked herbs.

The seasonings for this dish come from different times of the year, but they work extremely well together, and they are good to keep in the cupboard for other meals. In the spring, we ferment overwintered garlic shoots for about a month, then squeeze out the juice and add a bit of that to the tartare. In the late summer, we collect juniper berries while they are still green, then crush and infuse them with a strong-flavored vinegar, adding that to the garlic juice.

The rye bread in this dish is delicious. It's a recipe that I learned in Denmark—a traditional seeded rye done right. Make sure that you stir the rye berries at least once a day so that they all soften. I once broke a tooth on bread that was made too quickly! For the tartare, the bread slices should be toasted but still soft in the middle and just crisp around the edges.

**FOR THE JUNIPER VINEGAR**

2$\frac{1}{2}$ tablespoons/16 g fresh green juniper berries

1 cup/235 g high-quality cider vinegar

**FOR THE CURED EGG YOLKS**

2 cups/400 g kosher salt

$\frac{1}{2}$ cup/100 g granulated sugar

$\frac{1}{2}$ cup packed/100 g brown sugar

2 fresh egg yolks from Riley Starks

**FOR THE CURED VENISON**

(This is a percentage-by-weight curing process for a relatively small yield, so we're only furnishing gram measures.)

3.75 g granulated sugar

7.5 g sea salt

2 g mature pine needles

2 g parsley stems

1 fresh bay leaf

2.5 g fresh green juniper berries, crushed

2.5 g whole black peppercorns, crushed

1 wild venison heart (about 250 g)

**FOR THE VENISON TARTARE**

9 ounces/225 g wild venison shoulder meat,
    aged 6 to 7 weeks

Fermented green garlic brine (page 240)

8 thin slices of five-day rye bread (page 244)

3 tablespoons plus 1 teaspoon/50 g clarified high-quality
    unsalted butter

1 cup/25 g miner's lettuce leaves

### JUNIPER VINEGAR

Crush the juniper berries with a mortar and pestle. Combine the crushed berries and cider vinegar in a nonreactive container. Allow them to marry for a month, then use a fine-mesh sieve to strain out the solids.

### CURED EGG YOLKS

Mix together the salt and the white and brown sugars and pour three-quarters of the mixture into a container with a bottom that's about 4 x 2 inches (10 x 5 cm). Create a divot for each egg yolk.

Place 1 yolk in each divot, cover them with the remaining salt and sugar mixture, and let them cure for 24 hours in the refrigerator; they'll be slightly more firm than a dried apricot when done. Rinse the yolks under cold water and dry under a fan for 15 minutes, which should leave the exterior tacky.

Start the smoker. Cold smoke the yolks on a sheet pan for 3 hours, then store them at room temperature.

### CURED VENISON

Create a dry rub by combining the sugar, salt, pine needles, parsley stems, bay leaf, juniper berries, and black peppercorns. Cut the heart meat into 4 sections and coat them with the rub. Place the pieces in a covered container and allow the meat to cure in the refrigerator. After 3 days, scrape the rub from the meat with the back of a knife, then cold smoke it over alderwood for about 4 days, until it is fairly dry and hardened. Dry the meat overnight in a dehydrator set on low, removing it as soon as the texture is firm enough to create curls when grated with a Microplane.

### VENISON TARTARE

Trim the aged venison shoulder, cutting along muscle divisions, removing any bone, silverskin, veins, or dark tissue. Cut the meat into ¼-inch/.5 cm cubes and keep them cold in the refrigerator until serving.

### TO SERVE

Season the tartare with about a tablespoon of the juniper vinegar and a tablespoon of the fermented green garlic brine. Using a Microplane, grate about a tablespoon of the cured, dried meat onto the tartare, then stir it in. Toast both sides of the rye bread slices in a skillet with the clarified butter. Serve the tartare in a small, chilled bowl next to small plates with the toasted bread and the miner's lettuce. Grate about a quarter of a cured egg yolk onto each toast.

# SHIITAKE MUSHROOMS ROASTED OVER AN OPEN FLAME

When I first arrived on Lummi, it took some time to find my voice as a chef. Not because I felt inexperienced or unready to cook the food I knew I wanted to cook, but because the island was overwhelming and inspiring in an absolutely electric way. It takes a while to connect with your natural surroundings, follow their rhythms, and know what to serve when. Working at The Willows was my first opportunity to respond to the most spectacular and diverse ingredients I had ever seen.

These mushrooms taste amazing when grilled, and in a dish this simple, every element is important. You need very high-quality mushrooms, good finishing salt, and a hot wood fire.

The best shiitakes are grown outdoors. Exposure to sunlight and cooling at night combine to blister the mushroom cap and give it a more sturdy texture. Next in importance is freshness, and though they're not wild, mushrooms grown like this still have a season, and it is important to pick them at their peak. Their flavor diminishes very quickly after harvesting, so they should be picked and cooked on the same day. When grilled, the cap needs a near-black char, but the stem should be barely cooked through.

This recipe was something of a turning point in my own cooking, an embodiment of my style and the kind of food that I like to eat. It's simple but exquisite, a combination I strive for in all of our dishes.

SERVES 4

Grapeseed oil

1 pound/500 g fresh shiitake trimmings

2½ ounces/75 g dried shiitake mushrooms

Flake salt

8 just-picked medium shiitake mushrooms (about 140 g)

## SHIITAKE STOCK

Pour a thin coat of grapeseed oil into a medium saucepan and set it over medium-high heat. When the oil begins to smoke, sauté the shiitake trimmings until lightly browned, about 1 minute.

Pour 1 quart/1 L of water into the saucepan. Add the dried shiitakes, bring to a boil, then reduce the heat and simmer for 1 hour. Strain out and discard the solids. Season very gently, if at all, with salt; the stock should have a clean but not overpowering taste.

## GRILLED SHIITAKES

In a medium mixing bowl, coat the whole shiitakes with a tablespoon/15 g of grapeseed oil and season with salt. Place the mushrooms in a sous vide bag with 2 tablespoons of shiitake stock (the rest of the stock can be frozen for another use) and vacuum seal on high. Place the bag in the refrigerator and allow the mushrooms to marinate for an hour.

Prepare a fire for direct grilling. Remove the mushrooms from the bag and grill, cap down, over direct heat, until they begin to sweat and develop pronounced grill marks, about 4 minutes. Flip and grill the underside until the stem is softened and grill marks appear, about 1½ minutes.

## TO SERVE

Dust each mushroom with flake salt and serve immediately.

# SCRAPED ALBACORE
## WITH **A BROTH MADE FROM SMOKED BONES**

was woken one morning not too long ago by the loud sound of someone breathing into a microphone, followed by voices and murmurs that bounced up from the water and echoed through our house. It took a minute to come out of a dream and realize that I was hearing the Lummi tribe divers who use microphones to communicate with their boats while diving for sea cucumbers around the island.

The sea around Lummi Island is a cold mix of inland waters, water from the Pacific, and an abundance of water from mountain river estuaries. It creates a great biological diversity and makes it a hot spot for commercial fishing.

After coming to the island and working with top-notch fishermen, I realized what a large disconnect there is between chefs and commercial fishermen. Just-caught fish can be subjected to some amazingly poor treatment, being kicked around on boats and piled high into giant containers, but when you pay by the pound, it can be hard to find the boat that will catch fewer fish in order to give you better quality.

Once we have a just-caught fish, we wait. Fish this fresh is unusable for the first day or two after it is caught. Its body is stiff with rigor mortis, the pin bones impossible to remove. A good-sized tuna, like the one we use for this dish, will benefit from at least two days, if not four or five, of resting on ice to allow the flesh to relax.

SERVES 4

**FOR THE TUNA STOCK**

1 albacore tuna spine, any meat left from trimming scraped off

3 smoked and dried smelt (about 18 g) (page 236)

Grapeseed oil

10 dried shiitake mushrooms (about 15 g)

2 cups/500 g mussel stock (page 246)

Salt

**FOR THE TARTARE**

2 ounces/60 g albacore tuna loin

2 ounces/60 g albacore tuna belly

1 tablespoon/10 g grapeseed oil

**FOR SERVING**

1-inch/2.5 cm piece fresh horseradish root (about 35 g), peeled

2 teaspoons/3 g fresh parsley seeds

4 teaspoons/13 g grapeseed oil

## TUNA STOCK

Start your smoker and when it's ready, cold smoke the tuna spine on a half-sheet pan for 1 hour.

Soak the dried smelt in a bowl of cold water for 10 minutes, then drain the water and give the smelt a good rinse under the tap.

Once the tuna spine has finished smoking, heat a large skillet with a film of grapeseed oil over medium-high heat. Add the spine and brown it until golden and cooked through, about 2 minutes per side. Place the bones in a medium saucepan with the smelt and dried shiitakes and cover with the mussel stock and 2 cups/475 g water. Bring to a boil over medium heat, then reduce the heat and simmer, covered, until the stock has pleasant fish and smoke flavors, about 25 minutes.

Strain the stock into a 2-quart/2 L container, cool it over an ice bath, then season it with salt. Set aside ½ cup/ 125 g and freeze the rest for another use.

## TUNA TARTARE

Wash the tuna loin and belly in a 10 percent salt solution (1 quart/1 L water with 100 g salt) to remove any scales or blood.

Use a scallop shell to scrape each cut of raw fish into bite-sized or smaller pieces, discarding any bits of connective tissue, then mix the two cuts together and stir in 1 tablespoon grapeseed oil.

## TO SERVE

Place each portion of tuna in a small, chilled serving bowl. Grate about 1 teaspoon of horseradish over the tuna with a Microplane and sprinkle ½ teaspoon of fresh parsley seeds over the top. Drizzle with about 1½ tablespoons of tuna stock and 1 teaspoon of grapeseed oil.

I can't remember the first time I met Jeremy Brown, which is hard to believe because he is a merry, red-headed Cornishman, but I will never forget the first time I saw his fish. Jeremy has been fishing for The Willows for the last twelve years, long before I got here. He leaves Bellingham for about three days at a time on his small boat to catch whatever's biting, bringing a cooler or two of his catch to the kitchen when he's through. He handles each one gently, even going to the effort of tying a small string through the mouth of each fish he catches to carry them without strain. He also pressure bleeds the fish with a syringe and a small saltwater pump to flush out their circulatory systems. Removing as much blood as quickly as possible ensures the best flavor and texture from the flesh. Once that's done, the fish are weighed and packed in a cooler with crushed ice, with more ice in their belly cavities.

Through no fault of their own, chefs often don't realize that commercial fishing is a highly regulated business, not an open-season, all-you-can-catch buffet. There are limited openings strung out through different fishing zones over the course of a season (and sometimes those are only a few hours a year). In 2014, there were only two days when halibut could be fished in the Puget Sound, and each boat was allowed only a limited amount. The openings were spread out by a few weeks, but if you were to call a less-than-scrupulous fish supplier for the six weeks after the first opening, they would tell you about their great, just-caught local halibut.

We never know what Jeremy is going to bring in: some salmon, a few types of cod, some rockfish, a tuna, some mackerel, skate, or halibut. He'll text from his boat, sometimes even sending me a picture of his catch, and let me know what he's got. Each week, we take whatever he brings and figure out what to cook. Sometimes, it's all one type of fish, and other weeks, there might not be enough of any single type for the whole restaurant, and we'll use different fish at different tables.

Beyond this, getting to know our fishermen has given us a huge variety in the kinds of fish we can get. There are so many different fish that are caught, bought, and sold commercially, yet very few types trickle down to make it onto restaurant menus. Many great-tasting fish are seemingly known only to fishermen. When I told Jeremy that I was curious about the other types of fish he sees, he started to bring in all types of small fish, snapper-type fish, flounder, and even eel. One time he caught a giant angelfish that had apparently swum over all the way from Hawaii to Lummi Island.

# A PORRIDGE OF LOVAGE STEMS

had never cooked with lovage before moving to Denmark, but it's an amazing herb that grows rampant on Lummi. Here, we started by using the plant for several dishes, making infusions from the leaves and turning the seeds into capers, but we always had a large bin of lovage stems that ended up in the compost heap.

In the spring, lovage is tender and subtle, an almost entirely different plant than it is later in the year. This dish is best prepared before the plant bolts and flowers, when the stems are crisp, juicy, and pleasant to eat raw. The preparation resembles a risotto, with the lovage stems in place of rice, gradually softened while cooking in a smoky smelt stock. The consistency should be similar to risotto, too, with a creaminess achieved by mixing in a thick purée of blanched spinach and adding a knob of butter at the end. This porridge can easily be a stand-alone dish, but I tend to serve it alongside some caramelized shellfish, such as razor clams or small squid.

The smelt stock used in this porridge is a good one, something of a mother sauce here at The Willows. We clean, salt, smoke, and dry the small fish before infusing them into a broth with dried mushrooms.

SERVES 6 TO 8

3 scallions

⅓ cup/80 g smelt stock (page 247)

1 cup/90 g lovage stems, cut into ¼-inch/.5 cm lengths

1 cup/12 g lovage leaves, torn into pieces smaller than 1 inch/2.5 cm

½ cup/45 g rainbow chard stems, cut into ¼-inch/.5 cm cubes

½ cup/50 g rainbow chard leaves, torn into thumb-sized pieces

Salt

1 tablespoon/15 g high-quality unsalted butter

1 tablespoon/15 g spinach purée (page 247)

2 tablespoons/12 g chopped fermented green garlic (page 240)

Reduced white wine (page 251)

Verjus

Lovage oil (page 242)

Prepare a grill for direct grilling. Char the scallions over direct heat on the grill until well blackened, then finely chop them.

Bring the smelt stock to a boil in a medium saucepan over medium-high heat. Add the lovage stems and lovage leaves, along with the chard stems and chard leaves. Cook the mixture, stirring frequently, until only about a tablespoon of the liquid remains and the leaves are a nice, glowing green, 3 to 5 minutes. Remove from the heat, season with salt, and stir in the butter. Return to the heat and stir in the spinach purée until a nice, creamy sheen forms. Off the heat, stir in the scallions and fermented green garlic and season with reduced wine, verjus, and salt.

## TO SERVE

Put a spoonful of porridge in the center of a dish and drizzle it with lovage oil.

# FERMENTED TURNIPS WITH VERY AGED DUCK

Around the time that the reefnet gears and nets are brought in, the fish have gone north and the birds, eschewing a more traditional straight line, zigzag their way south through the San Juans. At the Inn, we start to serve a heartier menu that hopefully makes the sideways rain feel warmer.

We cook with birds from Koraley Orritt at Shepherd's Hill Farm on nearby Whidbey Island. She has raised several types of ducks and geese for us, often starting the baby chicks in her living room and eventually moving them out to her pasture. My current favorite is the small Khaki Campbell variety.

I like to push duck to the limits of dry aging, bringing it to that step just before it starts to go off. Strange as it sounds, I find this yields the most flavorful and best-textured meat. The cooking process removes any unpleasant off flavors the aged meat might have and produces a pure and distinct duck flavor that pairs beautifully with fruits and berries or fermented flavors. In this case, funk likes funk.

This past spring, we bought a flock of sixty live ducks, slaughtered them, and hung them in our walk-in cooler to age. After hanging the ducks for a week with their guts, we eviscerated them and basted them with a little rendered duck fat and continued to let them hang to further develop flavor and texture. Prior to cooking, we brine just the flesh overnight to rehydrate the meat a touch and tenderize the flesh while keeping the skin dry.

SERVES 4

**FOR THE DUCK**

1 whole, plucked Khaki Campbell duck (about 2.2 kg)

Grapeseed oil

Salt

2 tablespoons/28 g high-quality unsalted butter, roughly cut into $\frac{1}{2}$-inch/1 cm cubes

**FOR THE FERMENTED TURNIPS**

8 Hakurei turnips (about 130 g)

1 generous tablespoon/20 g salt

**FOR THE TURNIP LEAF SAUCE**

1 cup/235 g light vegetable stock (page 250)

1 bunch Hakurei turnip leafy tops (about 100 g)

$\frac{1}{2}$ teaspoon/2.5 g cold, high-quality unsalted butter

$1\frac{1}{2}$ teaspoons/7 g spinach purée (page 247)

Flake salt

High-quality cider vinegar

$\frac{1}{2}$ teaspoon/2 g grapeseed oil

**FOR THE BUTTER-GLAZED TURNIP LEAVES**

$\frac{1}{2}$ cup/100 g cold, high-quality unsalted butter

4 Hakurei turnip leaves, about 8 to 10 inches/20 to 25 cm long

## AGING THE DUCK

Trim any excess fat from around the neck and abdominal cavity of the duck. Tie the ends of the legs together tightly and hang the duck from its legs in a well-ventilated place where the temperature will consistently stay above freezing and below 45°F/7°C. Allow the duck to age, using a damp towel to wipe off any white mold as it appears. The duck will be ready in about 4 weeks, when the skin takes on an amber-pink tone and flesh touched with a finger takes a few seconds to return to its shape. Break down the duck, reserving all but the breasts for another use. Trim the fat around the breasts, leaving a neat, consistent ½-inch/1 cm of overhang around them. Soak the flesh side of the duck breast in a 7 percent salt brine for 1 hour. Chill until serving.

## FERMENTED TURNIPS

Clean the turnips, leaving them with about ½ inch/1 cm of stem and scraping off any stem fibers. Cut each turnip into 6 wedges. Place all of the wedges into a nonreactive container and cover with the salt mixed with 500 ml water (a 4 percent salt solution). Cover the turnips and liquid with parchment paper cut to fit the inside of the container and use a weight like a small plate on top of the paper to keep the turnips from coming in contact with the air. Cover the top of the container with cheesecloth and store in a space that stays between 55 and 75°F/13 and 24°C—the cooler end of that range being ideal. Ferment for 1 to 3 weeks. When done, the turnips will still have plenty of crunch and a nice, acidic tang. Cover and refrigerate, keeping the weight in place.

## TURNIP LEAF SAUCE

In a medium saucepan, bring the vegetable stock to a simmer over high heat. Put the turnip leaves into the blender, pour in the hot stock, and blend on high until it becomes a smooth liquid. Pour the sauce directly into a loaf pan set over ice to cool. Strain the cooled sauce through a fine-mesh sieve or a Superbag.

## DUCK BREASTS

Bring the breasts to room temperature. Preheat a large skillet over medium heat, coat the pan with a thin film of grapeseed oil, and sprinkle a pinch of salt onto the oil. Set the breasts in the skillet, skin-side down. Sprinkle a pinch of salt onto the flesh, followed by a thin coat of grapeseed oil (about ½ teaspoon per breast). Cook for about 7 minutes, or until much of the fat has rendered and the skin is crisp and has taken on a deep golden color. Drain out and discard any rendered fat that begins to pool as you cook.

Once the skin is crisp, wipe out the pan and place it over medium-low heat. Working quickly, add the butter cubes to the skillet, immediately followed by the duck breasts, flesh-side down, side by side. (If there are any signs of browning of the butter or the breasts, reduce the heat.)

After about 90 seconds, lean the breasts against the sides of the pan to cook the sides and ends of the flesh, cooking all visible parts that appear raw.

Remove the breasts from the heat and place them on a wire rack, skin-side down, and allow them to rest for at least 5 minutes but not more than 10. To re-crisp the skin before serving, place a skillet over medium-high heat, add a thin film of grapeseed oil, and when that's hot, add the breasts, skin-side down. Remove after 30 seconds.

Immediately trim any tough edges from the flesh and, cutting on the bias, trim ½ inch/1 cm from either end. Working at the same angle, cut the breast into 4 portions.

## BUTTER-GLAZED TURNIP LEAVES

Strain the brine from the fermented turnips into a medium saucepan and bring to a simmer over medium-high heat. Remove the pan from the heat and immediately add the ½ cup/100 g of butter. Once the butter is melted, blend the liquid with an immersion blender, stopping once an off-white emulsion with the consistency of heavy cream has formed. Bring the glaze to a gentle simmer and add the whole turnip leaves just long enough to wilt them, about 30 seconds. Pull the leaves out and set them in a strainer.

## TO SERVE

Heat the fermented turnips in the butter glaze over low heat until just warmed through.

Warm the turnip leaf sauce in a small saucepan over low heat, making sure it doesn't become warm enough to simmer. Stir in the ½ teaspoon/2.5 g of cold butter and the spinach purée and season it with salt and cider vinegar.

Lay a glazed turnip leaf onto each warmed serving plate and dust it with flake salt. Sprinkle the skin side of each duck breast piece with a tiny pinch of flake salt, then set a piece across the leaf. Mound 6 to 8 turnip wedges on the leaf.

Stir the ½ teaspoon/2 g of grapeseed oil into the turnip sauce, then spoon a little less than a tablespoon of the sauce onto the turnip leaf and serve immediately.

# BARELY WARMED PRAWNS WITH BARELY POACHED ROE

Spot prawn season runs from spring until fall, and most of ours are caught by Lummi tribe members. There are a few families who have sold their catch to The Willows for years, and they often deliver it by pulling their boats up onto the beach in front of the Inn. We'll buy a few hundred pounds at a time and keep them in our seawater tank a few days to make sure we have enough between catches.

Fresh, well-handled spot prawns have an incredible creamy and fresh flavor, almost like a langoustine, but better. I haven't found a way to eat spot prawns that I don't like, my favorite perhaps being grilled on the beach. We've prepared them about a dozen different ways, but this small dish is the best we've come up with at the restaurant to capture their flavor.

Making prawn butter is an amazing way to get the flavor to linger. We now make all sorts of flavored butters in the same fashion, using whichever parts don't end up as the centerpiece of a dish. We try to serve only the very best bits to our guests, and in this case, we can use prawn shells, undersized prawns, and any specimens that were mangled during peeling for the butter.

The method behind it involves extracting a stock from a paste, which we make using the whole shrimp. This does not result in the highest yield, but it creates an unbelievably pure flavor.

SERVES 4

20 large Haro Strait spot prawns with roe (about 600 g), whole with shells on

¼ cup/55 g high-quality unsalted butter

Flake salt

Scrape the roe from each prawn with a teaspoon and place the roe in a fine-mesh strainer and let it drain until serving. Place 5 of the smallest prawns—shells on—into the blender. Peel the remaining prawns, setting 4 large tails aside to poach, and place the remaining tails in the blender. Put all of the peeled shells and heads in a medium saucepan with the butter.

## PRAWN BUTTER

Cook the heads, shells, and butter over low heat, stirring occasionally, until the butter is a clear, bright orange, about 40 minutes. Strain the prawn butter through a Superbag and discard the solids.

## PRAWN STOCK

Bring a stockpot of water to a boil. While it heats, pulse the prawns in the blender and blend until puréed to a sherbet-like consistency. Pour the prawn paste into a sous vide bag and vacuum seal on low. (The bag should be slightly larger than you may think you need, as the paste has a tendency to expand during the vacuum process.) Simmer the bag in the stockpot for 1 hour. The contents will separate into paste and liquid. Reserve all of the liquid—this is the stock. When cool enough to handle, squeeze the paste through a Superbag to extract more stock and discard the paste.

## POACHED PRAWNS

Bring the prawn butter to 158°F/70°C in a small saucepan over medium heat. Remove the pan from the heat and cook the 4 reserved tails in the prawn butter until they begin to firm up and curl but still retain some translucence, 2 to 4 minutes.

## TO SERVE

Warm the prawn stock in a small saucepan over low heat.

Place a poached prawn tail and 2 roe sacs in the bottom of each small, warmed serving bowl. Dress the prawn and roe with about 2 tablespoons of hot prawn stock and about 1 tablespoon of the still-warm prawn butter, giving the bowl a gentle swirl to combine the liquids. Finish with a pinch of flake salt.

# A STIR-FRY OF WILD BEACH PEAS AND GIANT CLAMS

Tucked away behind Legoe Bay Road is a small shellfish farm that specializes in growing baby bivalves and is one of the few places in the world that raises geoduck seed. Part of the seeding process involves collecting very mature, wild geoducks from nearby beaches, and after they've been used for spawning, they are brought to The Willows.

Handling these enormous bivalves is a privilege that demands our full attention. The clams can be up to 150 years old, but instead of being as tough as leather, they're incredibly tender.

Beach peas grow rampant on our shores. Their flavor is similar to cultivated pea shoots, but with a succulent, slightly bitter character that goes well with the sweet brininess of geoduck and razor clams. They become something of a staple vegetable for us starting around April, the only time when they send out enough tender green shoots to make a dish like this possible. We make a salty, acidic dressing and season the stir-fried beach peas with grated dried smelt and scallops to deepen the flavors. At the end, the raw peas and their deep purple flowers help give this dish the look of the island's beaches in mid-spring.

SERVES 4

1 bunch beach peas (about 500 g)

4 large Quinault River razor clams (about 500 g)

1 cup/240 g high-quality heavy cream

1 cup/235 g clam stock (page 246)

Grapeseed oil

1 tablespoon plus 1 teaspoon/20 g high-quality unsalted butter

1 tablespoon/12 g reduced white wine (page 251)

Wash and dry the beach peas, trimming and composting anything not tender enough to eat raw (try a bite to be sure). Separate the pods, the leaves, and the tender tips. (You'll end up with fewer pods than leaves and tender tips.) In a bowl, create a mix of about one-third pods and two-thirds leaves and tender tips. Reserve some extra tips and discard any extra leaves.

Clean the razor clams, cut off and reserve the siphons, and reserve the feet. Cut the bodies in half lengthwise, then into pieces about an inch/2.5 cm wide.

Simmer the heavy cream in a small saucepan over low heat until reduced by half.

## ENHANCED CLAM SAUCE

Warm the clam stock in a small saucepan over low heat. Chop the siphons into ½- to 1-inch/1 to 2.5 cm pieces and press them dry between layers of paper towel. Place a small sauté pan over high heat and coat with a thin layer of grapeseed oil. Sear the siphons and the feet in batches until caramelized. Deglaze the sauté pan with about ¼ cup of the warmed clam stock and pour the siphons, feet, and remaining liquid into the saucepan with the clam stock. Cover the saucepan with plastic wrap and allow the liquid to steep for at least 20 minutes, then remove and discard the siphons and the feet.

Bring the infused clam stock to a simmer over medium-low heat. Stir in about 1½ tablespoons of the reduced cream and the butter. Buzz the sauce with an immersion blender and season with the reduced wine. It should have an intense but delicious chowder flavor.

Put a pair of skillets over high heat and coat the bottom of each with grapeseed oil. In one, sauté the beach pea mixture, adding a tablespoon of water to help steam them. Stir in a generous tablespoon of the enhanced clam stock and immediately remove the greens from the heat. The whole process should take about a minute. Sear the clam pieces in the other skillet until caramelized and just cooked through, then remove from the heat.

## TO SERVE

Layer the seared clams and sautéed beach peas onto each warmed serving plate. Spoon a teaspoon of enhanced clam stock over the top of each plate and garnish with the reserved tender beach pea tips.

# WHOLE ROASTED KOHLRABI
## WITH **CRUSHED CURRANTS** AND **MUSSELS**

While beluga caviar and foie gras represent a certain kind of luxury, to me, luxury is a cupful of salmonberry shoots, which is the product of hours spent picking the branch ends, then isolating enough for a dinner for thirty. Or a spoonful of nectar-rich anise hyssop flowers, each one no larger than the head of a pin. This is our take on rare and elusive ingredients and, to me, a more exciting form of luxury.

For this dish, we slowly roast whole kohlrabi in loads of butter and herbs, turning and basting it for hours. The kohlrabi almost chars on the outside and absorbs all of the flavors of the herbs while its own flavor deepens. The musky flavor of roasted kohlrabi is accented by the distinct flavors of currants, anise hyssop flowers, and mussels, which make for a simple but extraordinary combination.

SERVES 4

**FOR THE KOHLRABI**

2 small kohlrabi bulbs, trimmed of leaves and shoots (about 150 g)

Grapeseed oil

¾ cup/170 g high-quality unsalted butter, divided

8 sprigs thyme

4 sprigs rosemary

5 fresh bay leaves

5 sprigs parsley

1 shallot (about 45 g), roughly chopped

**FOR THE MUSSEL CREAM**

½ cup/120 g very cold mussel stock (page 246)

½ cup/120 g very cold high-quality heavy cream

**FOR THE GARNISH**

40 redcurrants, crushed with the back of a spoon

32 cilantro tips

4 teaspoons anise hyssop flowers

### KOHLRABI

Trim any bits of stalk from each kohlrabi bulb, leaving as much skin on as possible and creating a nice, smooth exterior. Slice off the very top and bottom to create flat surfaces to sear. Heat a film of grapeseed oil in a saucepan just large enough to accommodate the kohlrabies over medium-high heat. (If you have a pair of smaller saucepans, you could put one kohlrabi in each.) Sear the tops and bottoms of the kohlrabi bulbs until they have a dark auburn color, 6 to 7 minutes per side, then tip them to sear their sides.

Add a third of the butter to the pan to braise the bottoms of the kohlrabi bulbs and reduce the heat to a point where the butter is gently bubbling. If the butter moves past the brown butter stage and heads toward burning, pour it out and add new butter—you'll likely need to do this about 3 times during the cooking. Flip the bulbs every 20 minutes until they are cooked through and tender enough to give easily when poked with a cake tester. (Cooking time will vary between 2 to 4 hours.)

Tie the thyme, rosemary, bay leaves, and parsley sprigs into a bouquet with butcher's twine and allow it to cook in the braising butter along with the shallot for about 5 minutes. Discard the bouquet and allow the pot to rest off the heat while you make the mussel cream.

### MUSSEL CREAM

Combine the mussel stock and heavy cream in a metal mixing bowl and whip it vigorously for about 2 minutes until soft peaks form.

### TO SERVE

Slice the kohlrabies in half horizontally, set each half seared-side down on a small, warmed serving plate, and spoon a teaspoon of the braising butter over the top. Add a dollop of mussel cream on the side of the plate and garnish with the crushed currants, cilantro tips, and anise hyssop flowers.

# SLICES OF PORCINI MUSHROOMS
## WITH **GRILLED ASPARAGUS JUICES**

Once dinner is under way, we like having our chefs serve some dishes to our guests. It's a nice way to meet the people that have traveled so far to get here, and each cook tries to serve every table at least once. One night a few years ago, a young couple went bananas for a porcini dish that we served, and the guy asked me if I would like him to send me mushrooms that he collects. I must have told him to send some up, even though I didn't pay it too much thought.

A few days later, a thirty-pound box of the most pristine porcini I'd ever seen arrived on the kitchen steps with a note that said, "Thanks for dinner!" Two days after that, another huge box of perfect mushrooms arrived. The onslaught continued all through the fall season. When the porcinis started to slow down, he asked if we used matsutakes, then transitioned straight into sending box after box of matsutakes, all for credit toward his next meal. Since then, he has become one of our chief mushroom suppliers, sending dozens of mushroom varieties from all over the Pacific Northwest, always in the best condition I have ever seen. Working with Matt has allowed me to use types of mushrooms that I have only read about in foraging books and be introduced to many more that I might never have otherwise seen.

SERVES 4

**FOR THE PORCINI BUTTER**

¼ cup/60 g high-quality unsalted butter

2 ounces/60 g porcini mushrooms, roughly chopped

**FOR THE ASPARAGUS JUICE**

14 large asparagus spears (about 210 g), trimmed

Salt

**FOR THE PORCINI**

4 ounces/115 g porcini mushrooms

1 teaspoon/5 g spinach purée (page 247)

Salt

3 tablespoons/40 g woodruff oil

28 woodruff flowers

## PORCINI BUTTER

Preheat a sous vide water bath to 176°F/80°C and place the butter and the roughly chopped porcinis in a sous vide bag. Vacuum seal the bag on high and cook it in the water bath for 8 hours, then run the butter through a fine-mesh strainer. Discard the solids.

## ASPARAGUS JUICE

Prepare a hot fire for direct grilling, and when it's ready, grill the asparagus until deep grill marks appear, about 3 minutes. Flip and cook for about 3 more minutes. The spears should still be al dente. Immediately place them on a quarter-sheet pan and tightly wrap the pan with plastic wrap, letting them sit until they're cooked through, 5 to 10 minutes.

Run the grilled asparagus through a juicer and season the juice with salt to taste. You should have about ½ cup of juice.

## PORCINI

Clean all of the whole porcini by scraping their stems with a bird's-beak knife, then wipe the whole mushrooms down with a damp paper towel to give them a polished look. Cut the 2 best-looking porcini in half lengthwise and use a mandoline to slice those lengthwise about ¹⁄₁₆ inch/2 mm thick.

## TO SERVE

Combine the asparagus juice, spinach purée, and a pinch of salt in a small saucepan over low heat.

In another small saucepan, heat a tablespoon of porcini butter, a few drops of water, and a sprinkle of salt over low heat, then add the sliced porcini and cook, stirring gently, until they are meltingly tender and almost creamy.

Arrange the cooked, sliced mushrooms at the bottom of each serving plate. Spoon a quarter of the warmed asparagus juice and 2 teaspoons of woodruff oil onto each plate, along with about 7 woodruff flowers. At the table, use a truffle slicer to shave about 8 paper-thin slices of the whole, raw porcini on top of each dish.

# MANY TYPES OF WILD BERRIES
## IN A BROTH OF HERBS AND GRASSES

like to see, taste, and collect what's growing wild on my walk to work in the morning. It's a chance to clear my head before the workday begins and to dream about a new dish or technique.

The variety of wild edibles on the island is so huge that I constantly discover new types of plants that I must have walked by a hundred times before. I like their direct flavor and try to feature a heavy dose of them on every menu.

There are so many wild edibles growing here, it's no wonder that the island was once guarded berry-picking grounds for the Lummi tribe.

When you live on a small island, collecting plants from the wild is more like stewarding than harvesting. We have to care for and look after the plants that we use for cooking so that as many or more grow back the following year. That might mean collecting the berries that we would like to use, then spending a few minutes clearing out any other plants that are competing with them for light.

I am always amazed by the way plants burst to life after a long winter. Angelica is usually one of the first, along with nettles and salmonberries, and they are followed by a barrage of green leaves and herbs of all different flavors. The days get longer quickly in the spring, and before long, we are overrun with dozens of wild berries and all sorts of edible plants. We follow along as the different plants mature, first on the west side of the island and then to the east, before moving up the mountainside to near-alpine meadows.

Much of what we serve is stark in its simplicity, but sometimes nature supplies us with such abundance that it would be unfair to our guests to exercise too much restraint.

SERVES 4

**FOR THE GARNISH**

16 lemon balm tips

16 angelica flowers

16 oregano flowers

16 wild geranium flowers

**FOR THE GRASS BROTH**

1 ounce/25 g wheatgrass, roughly chopped

½ ounce/13 g fresh dill

½ cup/35 g parsley leaves

2 tablespoons plus 2 teaspoons/40 g Stock syrup (page 256)

2 tablespoons plus 2 teaspoons/40 g verjus

¾ ounce/22 g parsley purée (page 247)

**FOR THE BERRIES**

4 thimbleberries

8 wild raspberries

8 trailing blackberries

8 salmonberries

12 red huckleberries

16 redcurrants

4 Indian plums

4 gooseberries

4 blueberries

4 salal berries

4 aronia berries

Parsley oil (page 242)

## GRASS BROTH

In a blender, combine ¾ cup/190 g water with the wheatgrass, dill, parsley leaves, and stock syrup and blend on high until the liquid is puréed, with just small bits of herbs, about 15 seconds. Pass the liquid through a Superbag and skim the foam from the top of the strained liquid. Season with the verjus (you may need a little more or less than the called-for amount) and stir in the parsley purée to thicken the mixture.

## TO SERVE

Arrange a mix of berries in the bottom of each chilled serving bowl. Drizzle about a tablespoon of the grass broth and a few drops of parsley oil over the berries and garnish with the herbs and flowers.

# GRILLED LEAVES OF CARAFLEX CABBAGE
## WITH **LEMON VERBENA**

I was blown away when I first tasted cone-shaped Caraflex cabbage in 2011. Every time I eat it, it is amazing to me that any other type of cabbage would ever be grown.

Caraflex has a juicy, crisp texture and a mild, sweet flavor, and the leaves are surprisingly delicious and tender when eaten raw. The large cabbages grow quickly and flower early in the year, whirling into dense cones that we can start using by late May, roasting or grilling the heads to amplify their flavor.

I like to poach the quartered heads of cabbage in butter with sprigs of verbena and then grill them before separating the leaves and folding them over each other. For this dish, we lighten the full flavor of charred cabbage with a bright sauce made from homemade rhubarb wine and verbena.

SERVES 4

**FOR THE GARNISH**
20 small verbena leaves

**FOR THE VERBENA SAUCE**
1 cup/240 g rhubarb wine (page 237)
1 cup/225 g high-quality unsalted butter, cut into ¾-inch/2 cm cubes
1 cup/60 g lightly packed verbena leaves
Salt
Reduced white wine (page 251)
1 tablespoon/15 g spinach purée (page 247)

**FOR THE CABBAGE**
½ medium Caraflex cabbage (about 225 g)
¼ cup/55 g high-quality unsalted butter
1 sprig verbena
1 teaspoon/5 g grapeseed oil
Flake salt

## VERBENA SAUCE

Reduce the rhubarb wine in a small saucepan over medium heat until only about 2 tablespoons remain. Whisk in the butter, a cube at a time, then remove the pan from the heat. Pour the liquid into a blender, add the verbena leaves, and blend on medium until the leaves are liquefied. Allow the mixture to steep in a warm spot for 1 hour. Strain it through a Superbag into another small saucepan and season it with salt and reduced white wine. Stir in the spinach purée.

## CABBAGE

Heat a sous vide water bath to 185°F/85°C. Cut the cabbage half in half, pole to pole, leaving 2 quarters. Place the quarters in a sous vide bag with the butter and verbena and vacuum seal the bag on high. Cook the cabbage in the water bath until it's tender, about 2 hours. Drop the bag into an ice bath until the cabbage is cold. Drain the liquid from the bag, remove the cabbage, and pat it dry. Discard the verbena sprig.

Prepare a fire for direct grilling. Toss the cabbage quarters in the grapeseed oil, then grill their flat sides until they are deeply browned. Remove the cabbage from the heat and separate the individual leaves from the core—you'll only use about 20 of the thicker, sturdier leaves. Place those on a parchment-lined tray and sprinkle them with flake salt.

## TO SERVE

In small, warmed serving bowls, fold and curl the cabbage leaves to give the dish a bit of height. Pour 2 tablespoons of verbena sauce around the bottom of each bowl and garnish the top of the cabbage with the verbena leaves.

# WARM BLUEBERRIES
## AND **AN ICE CREAM MADE FROM SWEET WOODRUFF**

This is one of my favorite desserts—the combination of a hot, malty stew of blueberries and cool woodruff ice cream works very well together. I love creating a balance between sweet and crunchy, hot and sticky, and cool and fresh.

The ice cream is made with both fresh and dried woodruff, making it a dish that can only really be made in late summer, after we have harvested the first trimmings of woodruff for drying and it has regrown, flowering for the last time before it goes to seed in the early fall. It is important to use very high-quality milk whenever you make ice cream, as it is the main ingredient, and to treat the ice cream base as you might a fresh herb sauce—working quickly and keeping it very cold—to keep the flavors bright. Similarly, berries lose their flavor very quickly after picking, particularly in the case of blueberries; their texture also suffers as they age. It is important to make the extra effort to use the best berries available. For us, this means driving to a nearby farm several times a week to get berries picked that morning.

SERVES 4

**FOR THE MALT COOKIES**

2 fresh egg yolks from Riley Starks

1 tablespoon plus ½ teaspoon/15 g dark syrup (page 256)

1 scant tablespoon/15 g squid ink

1¼ cups/125 g sifted all-purpose flour

¼ cup/25 g sifted cornstarch

1 tablespoon/10 g malt powder

¼ teaspoon/.75 g kosher salt

½ cup plus 2 tablespoons/125 g high-quality unsalted butter, at room temperature

3 tablespoons/30 g granulated sugar

**FOR THE WOODRUFF ICE CREAM**

3 cups/790 g whole milk

½ cup/125 g heavy cream

½ cup/105 g granulated sugar

3 tablespoons plus 1 teaspoon/65 g corn syrup

6 cups/70 g roughly chopped woodruff sprigs, plus 24 sprigs for garnish

2 tablespoons/30 g spinach purée (page 247)

2 sheets bronze leaf gelatin

2 tablespoons dark syrup (page 256)

1 cup/175 g just-picked blueberries

Verjus

½ cup/50 g meringue (page 255)

## MALT COOKIES

Stir the yolks, dark syrup, and ink together in a small bowl. In a medium bowl, combine the flour, cornstarch, malt powder, and kosher salt. Cut the butter into ½-inch/1 cm cubes, then place the cubes in a stand mixer with the sugar and mix on medium with the paddle attachment until combined, about 1 minute. Add the yolk mixture and mix on medium until combined, occasionally stopping to scrape down the sides.

Add the flour mixture to the mixer bowl and mix on low, stopping as soon as the entire mixture is uniformly dark. Portion the dough into hunks of about ½ cup/100 g each. (This recipe makes about 8 portions of the dough, and anything not being used immediately can be frozen at this point.)

Preheat the oven to 300°F/150°C. Put the portions of dough between two Silpat mats or layers of parchment paper. Roll the dough as thin as possible without creating holes and freeze it until the dough takes on a puttylike consistency and no longer sticks to both sides of the Silpat or parchment, 5 to 10 minutes.

Remove the top Silpat or parchment and put the flattened dough and the Silpat or parchment beneath it onto a half-sheet pan and bake until crisp, about 20 minutes. Let cool, then crush with your fingers into pieces no larger than ½ inch/1 cm.

## WOODRUFF ICE CREAM

Whisk together the milk, cream, granulated sugar, and corn syrup in a large saucepan. Bring it to just below a simmer (it should be steaming, not boiling) over medium heat.

Place the woodruff sprigs in the blender, then remove the milk mixture from the heat and pour it over the woodruff. Mix until thoroughly blended and only tiny flecks of the leaves remain, about 30 seconds. Let the mixture steep for 5 minutes and strain it through a fine-mesh strainer, then through a Superbag. Whisk in the spinach purée to give the liquid a more saturated green color and season it with more granulated sugar if necessary. Pour about 2 tablespoons of the liquid into a small saucepan and the rest into a Pacojet beaker.

Soak the gelatin sheets in cold water until they bloom— becoming hydrated and completely supple—5 to 10 minutes. Gently hand-squeeze the sheets to expel any water pockets and place them in the saucepan with the woodruff liquid. Melt the gelatin over low heat, then whisk it into the Pacojet beaker with the woodruff liquid. Freeze the mixture and keep it in the freezer until serving.

## TO SERVE

Process the ice cream in the Pacojet.

Heat the dark syrup in a small saucepan over medium heat and reduce it until only about 2 teaspoons remain. Reduce the heat to low, add the blueberries to the saucepan, and stir gently but quickly to coat the berries in the dark syrup glaze until they're just warmed through, 20 to 30 seconds. Season them with a few drops of verjus.

Dot each dessert plate with 3 domes of meringue (about ¼ inch/.5 cm across), then gently toast their exterior with a blowtorch. Put a cluster of berries on the plate, then a scant tablespoon of the crumbled malt cookies over the top of the berries. Place ½ teaspoon of crumbled cookies in a line to the side of the berries. Tuck a few woodruff sprigs into the spaces between the berries and set a scoop of the ice cream on the line of cookie crumbs.

# BUNDLES OF ROMANO BEANS
# ROASTED OVER OREGANO SPRIGS

Romano beans are at their best before they are fully grown and getting a bit stringy. The beans must be amazing raw in order to be amazing cooked, and we simply bundle them around sprigs of oregano and grill them over hot coals. When the outside has a good char, we pull them from the grill and baste them with a flavorful herb sauce and lardo.

SERVES 4

**FOR THE HERB SAUCE**

1/2 cup/15 g marjoram leaves

1/2 cup/15 g oregano leaves

1/2 cup/15 g parsley leaves

1/2 cup/120 g grapeseed oil

1 anchovy fillet

Salt

Verjus

Fermented green garlic brine (page 240)

**FOR THE GRILLED ROMANO BEANS**

1 1/2 ounces/40 g frozen Mangalitsa lardo

8 ounces/240 g Romano beans

8 sprigs oregano

Grapeseed oil

**HERB SAUCE**

Crush the marjoram, oregano, parsley, oil, and anchovy with a mortar and pestle to form a thick paste. Season the sauce with salt, verjus, and fermented green garlic brine and immediately transfer it to the refrigerator, with a piece of parchment cut to fit directly on the surface of the sauce to prevent any discoloration.

**GRILLED ROMANO BEANS**

Grate the frozen lardo into a medium mixing bowl. Wearing plastic gloves, work it into a smooth paste with your hands. Transfer the lardo into a small piping bag and allow it to warm to room temperature.

Trim the stem ends from the Romano beans and tie them with the oregano sprigs into 4 tight bundles with kitchen twine.

Prepare a grill for direct grilling, brush the bundled beans with grapeseed oil, and grill them, rotating occasionally. When the beans are just cooked through, remove them from the heat, untie, and discard the oregano.

**TO SERVE**

Pipe a quarter of the lardo into the center of each bundle of beans, turning each bundle to dress it with the lardo. Plate the bundles and nap each plate with a full tablespoon of the herb sauce.

# SMOKED SOCKEYE SALMON

Smoked salmon is a pillar of cuisine in the Pacific Northwest, and the region even has its own style of smokehouse. Most locals know how to smoke salmon, and those who don't tend to know scores of people who do.

When I first arrived at The Willows, I knew that I wanted to serve perfect smoked salmon. Not long after I started working here, Robert Keller, a Lummi Island local and friend of The Willows, stopped by to use our vacuum sealer to bag some salmon he had just smoked. He gave me a bite and it was easily the best that I'd ever tried. I tagged along with him the next time he smoked a batch so I could see how well-made smoked salmon is made.

I learned that I had a lot to learn.

There are big differences in the way each type of salmon smokes. To me, sockeye works particularly well and is what we serve nightly; the flavor and texture are sublime if you do it just right. Brining and then drying the fish is a key step that wicks some of the water from the flesh and makes each flake densely packed with flavor.

Smoking fish is much easier on cold, dry winter days than on hot or rainy days when the smokehouse needs more attention. Temperature, humidity, and barometric pressure all play a part in how the salmon reacts to the smoke. A gentle smoke tastes much different than a heavy smoke, so I tend to smoke very lightly over longer time periods. Finally, our smoked salmon must not be baked—if the temperature in the smoker gets too hot, the sashimi-like texture that I love turns into something akin to baked salmon.

We get all of our salmon for the year from right here on the island in the span of a short, three-week season, all of it coming from the reefnetters just off of Lummi's shore. The reefnet salmon, which can include pink, silver, and chum salmon as well as the sockeye, are all exceptional fish. Since their ultimate destinations are far up British Columbia's Fraser River and its tributaries, they are at an early stage of their journey when they reach Lummi and still have large amounts of stored fat. They are all handled individually, live-bled, and immediately slush-iced.

The difference between a reefnet fish and a gill net or purse seine fish is obvious immediately upon cutting into it. The reefnet fish is bright, clean, and virtually bloodless, while the flesh of the fish caught with other methods has a dark, dull color. The difference in flavor follows a similar parallel. Reefnet fish are fresh, firm, and clean, while the other fish have an unmistakable fishiness and a slight flabbiness, even when fresh, that I've come to identify with the blood they've retained.

I've been smoking salmon just about every day since I first met Robert, gradually tweaking and improving my technique the whole time. My salmon now is quite different from his, but I still like to think of what we serve as a piece of traditional Northwest smoked salmon, perfected by daily practice.

**FOR THE SALT BRINE**

1 cup/200 g kosher salt

**FOR THE GLAZE**

½ cup/115 g high-quality unsalted butter

½ cup plus 1 tablespoon packed/125 g brown sugar

¼ cup/55 g verjus

Salt

**FOR THE SALMON**

2 Lummi Island Wild sockeye salmon fillets
    (about 760 g total), pin bones removed

### SALT BRINE

In a large resealable container, whisk the salt into 1 quart/1 L of hot water until it's completely dissolved, then store the brine in the refrigerator until cold.

### GLAZE

Melt the butter in a medium saucepan over low heat. Once the butter begins to foam, whisk the brown sugar in slowly. Let it heat for 5 minutes to ensure all of the sugar has melted. Whisk in the verjus and add salt to taste, then cover the pan and reserve in the refrigerator.

### SALMON

Trim the collar, belly, and tail end to create a form that's rectangular seen from above and a uniform, flattened "D" shape from the side. About a third of the fillet will be trimmed away as scrap.

Cut individual portions that are about ¾ inch/2 cm wide and place them in the container with the salt brine. Cut a sheet of parchment paper to fit the inside of the container, then lay it on top of the water to keep the salmon out of contact with the air. Brine for 37 minutes, then drain and quickly rinse with fresh water.

Line a half-sheet pan with a double layer of kraft paper. The fish will smoke right on the paper, so make sure that the paper is cut small enough to fit inside the smoker. Set the fish on the pan, skin-side down, making sure each piece is positioned squarely upright and allowing plenty of space for air to circulate between each portion. Place the fish, uncovered, in the refrigerator to dry overnight, as close to the fan as possible.

The following day, start the smoker and set the salmon, still on the kraft paper but without the tray, into the smoker and away from the heat. As it smokes, make sure the fish is not sweating too much or drying out. (If it is, remove the salmon from the smoker until the smoker is cooler.) It should become slightly taut on the exterior, and the color will intensify while the cut edges become slightly white and translucent.

After about 2½ hours, warm the glaze over low heat until it reaches 150°F/65°C—a temperature that's just warm enough to spread thickly, but not so warm that it cooks the fish. Remove the salmon from the smoker and allow it to cool to room temperature, then apply a thick layer of glaze with a basting brush. Smoke the fish for another hour, then remove the salmon from the kraft paper using a small offset spatula, sliding the spatula blade between the flesh and the skin, leaving the skin on the kraft paper. Brush the top of each portion with a second coat of glaze.

### TO SERVE

Plate and serve immediately. If not serving the fish straight from the smoker, preheat the oven to 200°F/93°C and warm the salmon in the oven for 4 minutes before serving.

* The process for our smoked cod (and the other fish we smoke) is very similar. We use a 1¼-pound/580 g black cod fillet, slicing the portions on the bias. The brining time should be shorter—about 6 minutes—and the fish should only smoke for about 3 hours on individual 6 x 6-inch/15 x 15 cm sheets of kraft paper. The pin bones are more easily removed after smoking, and there's no glazing.

# BRAISED SEAWEED
## WITH **DUNGENESS CRAB** AND **BROWN BUTTER**

Diving into the waters off Lummi is a bracing experience—you might want to have a few drinks before you take the plunge. After a few moments in the shockingly cold water, your body becomes numb, though you swear you can almost feel ice crystals forming in your spine. In a good way. In the summer, the water is just a few degrees warmer than it is in the winter, but it is lit up with phosphorescent plankton that trace glowing circles following your arms and legs on a midnight swim.

The ulva seaweed that we use for this dish lies dormant all winter, before it slowly starts to come back in the spring. By the end of summer, it grows like grass and we can pull huge sheets off the rocks. If this dish is in your section at the restaurant, an important part of your prep for the day and week is to keep track of the tide charts and when the best time to harvest the seaweed might be. If several days of higher tides are coming in, you might need to do a bit of wading.

The water in and around the Puget Sound is also rich with crustaceans. Next to the ferry dock on the mainland is a Lummi fish merchant. Their crab traps pile up down the length of their dock on the days that are closed to fishing. If there are no traps on the dock, I know I can probably get fresh crab the following day. At the restaurant, we have a large seawater tank just outside the kitchen where we can hold huge numbers of crab and spot prawns in pristine condition for up to a month, feeding them some clams when they get hungry. Having the large tank helps us to work directly with the fishermen and coordinate with their regulated season of openings and quotas, while giving us a bit of a buffer in case we get a week of foul weather and they can't fish.

When making this intensely flavored dish, it is important to use live crab and to clean them thoroughly. This dish is very tasty—brown butter and crab go remarkably well together—but it's one that is not made better by serving more of it.

2 live Dungeness crabs (about 1.8 kg)

2 cups/500 g mussel stock (page 246)

4 ounces/100 g fresh ulva seaweed

¼ cup/55 g high-quality unsalted butter, browned

¼ cup/10 g freshly grated horseradish

1 tablespoon/10 g grapeseed oil

Salt

## CRAB

Fill a stockpot with 5 quarts/4.75 L of seawater (if you can't get seawater, you can use freshwater mixed with 1¾ cups/175 g kosher salt) and bring to boil. Remove the pot from the heat, add one of the crabs, cover tightly, and let it cook off the heat for 36 minutes. Place the crab on ice and let it chill until cool enough to handle. Pick the crab clean—it should yield about 1⅓ cups/225 g crabmeat. Set the bits of shell in a large saucepan and place the crabmeat in a container on a bed of crushed ice.

## CRAB STOCK

In the large saucepan, crush the shell and the other live crab with the blunt end of a rolling pin until all shell fragments are smaller than 1 square inch/2.5 square cm, then pour the mussel stock over the top. Cover the saucepan tightly with plastic wrap and simmer for 5 minutes. Remove the pan from the heat and let the stock steep, still covered, for another 15 minutes, then strain it through a fine-mesh strainer.

## SEAWEED

Dry the ulva seaweed overnight in a dehydrator (it should be crisp enough to break). Place the dried seaweed in a 4-quart/3.75 L container and add 3½ quarts/3.5 L of just-boiled water. Let it soak for 30 minutes. Drain and repeat with fresh, just-boiled water for another 30 minutes. Drain the seaweed for 30 minutes, then put it into a medium saucepan and add half of the crab stock. Simmer for 30 minutes, then allow it to marinate for 2 hours, covered, in the refrigerator.

## TO SERVE

Reheat the seaweed and the stock it was marinating in over low heat. In a separate small saucepan over low heat, warm the remaining crab stock with the brown butter. In a third pot, also over low heat, combine the crabmeat with the freshly grated horseradish and grapeseed oil. Use salt to adjust the seasoning for both the seaweed and the crabmeat.

Divide the crab evenly between each small, shallow warmed serving bowl and cover the crab with a layer of seaweed. Stir the brown butter and crab stock mixture and spoon 3 teaspoons of it over each dish.

# SUMMER FLOWERS FROM THE FARM

Spending time in our small garden has shown me a new world of ingredients, tastes, and textures that have been a dream to explore. The sight of our small farm bursting with life in the summer is always encouraging to me. The vibrancy of the growing plants and the bright colors of their flowers meets a warm breeze, the buzzing of bugs, and the sound of the sea. I walk between the farm's rows of produce almost every day, snipping off a leaf or twig as I go, waiting for inspiration from the bright flavors. Much of the time, the clues are obvious, almost screaming, that a plant is at a stage of flavor so amazing that it is a near masterpiece in itself. This is particularly noticeable with some of the herb and vegetable flowers, which explode with flavor and make for an exciting shared plate.

I have become very aware of plant habits, life cycles, and even their likes and dislikes. "Seasonal" becomes a whole new word that doesn't really describe a set time of the year and certainly not four quarters of a year. Plants don't naturally fruit for long periods: they throw all their energy into reproducing, and generally speaking, a given plant will only have ripe fruit or vegetables for a few weeks if you're lucky. Here, the four seasons of the year can feel more like thirty!

Mary von Krusenstiern is a remarkable farmer. She runs the farm like a Michelin-starred kitchen and is every bit as curious and excited as I am. We grow 100 percent of the produce for the ten months that The Willows is open, which makes for a challenging proposal, but one that's possible if we're disciplined. Mary and I meet each day, including at the beginning and end of every season. Around November, we review our notes to see which plants grew well and which varieties we liked the best, and we organize the order for the coming year's seeds. Even though we are fairly far north, we rarely get much snow, and the ground doesn't usually freeze. Even in the winter months when the kitchen is closed, we can continue to grow and overwinter plants. We do battle with a lack of sunlight, though...plants and people alike. It is almost always overcast in the winter, and the sun sets around three in the afternoon. Sometimes, a week will go by with no actual sun sighting. With that little light, plants don't grow as much as they simply maintain. They're not growing or dying. They're just waiting. At the first hint of spring, however, they explode back to life.

We grow as many varieties of any given plant as possible, and each year we have a number of experimental crops, always looking for new plants to cook with. What is usually considered the edible part of the plant is often just an abbreviation of the whole. The stems, flowers, seeds, leaves, and roots can all be used.

**FOR THE NASTURTIUM FLOWER SAUCE**

5 ounces/150 g nasturtium flowers

1 tablespoon/17 g high-quality cider vinegar

1½ teaspoons/8 g Dijon mustard

¼ cup/25 g crushed ice

½ cup/110 g cold grapeseed oil

Salt

**FOR THE SALAD**

1 pound/500 g pattypan squash

Grapeseed oil

Salt

Verjus

12 assorted basil leaves, such as Genovese, Thai, dark opal,
    purple ruffles, and spicy globe

12 nasturtium leaves, about 1 inch/2.5 cm across

20 perfect nasturtium flower petals

8 zucchini blossoms, each torn into about 8 strips

**NASTURTIUM FLOWER SAUCE**

Combine the nasturtium flowers, cider vinegar, Dijon, and ice in a blender. Blend on low until everything begins to catch in the blender, then switch to high to liquefy. Add the grapeseed oil slowly, as if making a mayonnaise, and blend until completely smooth, about 1 minute.

Strain the mixture through a fine-mesh strainer into a small container on ice. Season sparingly with salt and refrigerate until ready to serve.

**SALAD**

Two hours before serving, prepare a grill for direct grilling. Coat the squash with oil and grill it whole, turning frequently, until the skin is blistered and charred and the center is completely soft. Remove it from the heat and once cool, crack the squash in half (like an egg), drop the halves into a Superbag, and squeeze the juice into a large bowl. Season the juice with salt and verjus, then add the basil, nasturtium leaves, nasturtium flower petals, and zucchini blossoms to the bowl and toss to dress them in the roasted squash juice.

**TO SERVE**

Place the dressed salad next to a tablespoon of nasturtium flower sauce on each small serving plate.

# ESCAROLE DRESSED WITH HOMEMADE CAPERS

Whole braised heads of escarole glazed in roasted onion juices makes for a winter entrée that many find surprising. It is eye opening to some customers who are accustomed to large portions of steak to have such a savory and satisfying entrée made from just a few vegetables. Yet this dish eats more like a piece of steak than a salad; it's savory and satisfyingly full of umami flavor. I like to roll the glazed escarole halves in homemade capers and tiny thyme leaves before placing each on the plate, unaccompanied.

SERVES 4

### FOR THE GARNISH

28 thyme tips

12 wild geranium flowers

4 teaspoons/13 g thyme oil (page 242)

4 teaspoons/12 g elderflower capers (page 241)

1½ ounces/40 g thinly sliced apple capers (page 241)

### FOR THE ONION SAUCE

2 cups/475 g onion stock (page 248), divided

A knife point (very tiny pinch) of xanthan gum

Verjus

High-quality cider vinegar

### FOR THE ESCAROLE

Grapeseed oil

2 large heads escarole (about grapefruit size), halved lengthwise

## GARNISH

Pick the thyme tips and wild geranium blossoms into ice water and store them in a damp paper towel–lined container until serving.

## ONION SAUCE

Pour half of the onion stock into a very small saucepan. Place an immersion blender in the pan, start blending, and slowly incorporate the xanthan gum, then bring to a simmer and keep warm over low heat. Skim the surface with a strainer and season with a few drops of verjus and cider vinegar.

## ESCAROLE

Heat a large skillet over high heat, add a thin layer of grapeseed oil, and when the oil shimmers, add the escarole halves, flat-side down. Cook until nicely charred, about 2 minutes. Reduce the heat to medium, drain any oil from the skillet, and add the remaining half of the onion stock. Allow the escarole to braise for 3 minutes, then flip it and cook for another 3 minutes, constantly basting the escarole as it cooks.

Remove the escarole from the skillet and set it on a paper towel, flat-side up.

## TO SERVE

Place a wedge of escarole on each plate and nap it with 2 tablespoons of the onion sauce and 1 teaspoon of thyme oil. Garnish with the thyme tips, geranium flowers, and elderflower and apple capers.

# DRIED MIRABELLE PLUM SKINS, A CANDY MADE FROM ROSEMARY

n the late summer, wild plums ripen all over the island during a very short season. These plums can be red or yellow, and they have larger pits and thicker skin than cultivated plums. We collected them and experimented, working our way toward a plum dessert. One trial had the plums stewing uncovered in a pot, and we found that the skins floating to the top were exposed to the air and became leathery, with a concentrated flavor. After drying those skins a touch more in front of the hearth, they were perfect.

SERVES 4

16 Mirabelle plums (about 1 kg)

Stock syrup (page 256)

1 (10-inch/25 cm) square rosemary candy (page 257), broken into $\frac{1}{2}$-inch/1 cm shards

## PLUM SKINS

Quarter 3 of the best-looking plums and discard the pits. Carefully slice the skins from each quarter, leaving them with about ⅛ inch/3 mm of flesh. Cover and refrigerate the skins and place the scrap in a medium metal mixing bowl.

## PLUM PURÉE

Pit and roughly chop the remaining plums. Place about 2½ cups/375 g of the chopped plums in the blender (reserving the remaining chopped plums) and blend on high until completely liquefied, about 30 seconds. Push the liquid through a sieve with a rubber scraper. Season the purée with stock syrup and reserve it in the refrigerator.

## PLUM GRANITA

Add the remaining roughly chopped plums to the mixing bowl with the scrap from the skins and cover the bowl tightly with 3 layers of plastic wrap. Half fill a stockpot with water, bring it to a boil, and set the mixing bowl over it. Let the plums cook with the water simmering beneath until the plum liquid is tinted red and the flesh is barely holding together, about 2 hours. Strain the plum liquid through a Superbag into another mixing bowl, discarding any solids. Season this jus with stock syrup to balance acidity and sweetness. Pour the jus into a 9 x 5 x 3-inch (23 x 13 x 7.5 cm) loaf pan, cover, and freeze.

Scrape the surface of the frozen jus in a crosshatch pattern with the tines of a fork to create the granita. Remove the granita from the pan and reserve it in the freezer in a cold, empty container.

## TO SERVE

Preheat the oven to 300°F/150°C. Spread the plum skins, flesh-side down, across a baking sheet lined with a Silpat mat or parchment paper and heat them in the oven until the plum skin wrinkles, about 6 minutes.

Place a tablespoon of plum purée in the center of each small, chilled serving bowl. Cover the purée with 3 tablespoons of granita. Top the granita with 3 plum skins and a few shards of rosemary candy.

# WHOLE WHEAT BREAD AND CHICKEN DRIPPINGS

Up at Nettles Farm, Riley Starks raises chickens for eggs, and at times I think that there might be as many as 200 birds up there on his little plot. They roam around the farm, turning over the dirt a little as they go. We send up organic kitchen scraps to help feed them.

When chickens are about a year and a half old, their egg production slows and they become known as "retired layers." These are the birds we use to create what we call "chicken pan drippings," a dish that we serve with really good bread and butter.

The bread we serve it with is something I have been making every day since I arrived, over and over, constantly working to master it. We use 100 percent whole wheat flour and coarse rye from a local farm that mills them for us at the beginning of each week.

This recipe is unique in that we pre-ferment more than half the dough while we soak the other part of the flour overnight for an extra-long autolyse (the resting period between mixing and kneading). We get the best results adding a small amount of commercial yeast during mixing, which gives the whole wheat dough a bit of a boost. After the initial mix, the dough is slowly proofed overnight before being shaped and baked.

Our bread oven is a hearth with thick stone walls. It takes an entire morning of firing to heat it, and then another hour before the heat evens out enough for us to put the loaves inside. We can fit exactly eleven large loaves of bread into the oven if perfectly placed. We then spray a light misting of water inside to fill the oven with steam and seal the door. We bake the bread quickly to achieve a crisp, dark-brown crust and custard-like crumb. After the loaves have cooled, I like to toast them in the oven just before serving to re-crisp the crust and heat them through.

## WHOLE WHEAT BREAD

YIELDS 1 LOAF

2 cups/275 g hard red winter wheat flour

1½ cups/275 g 100% hydration coarse rye starter

¾ teaspoon/2 g fresh cake yeast

1 tablespoon plus ¼ teaspoon/11 g salt

¼ cup/35 g rye flour

¼ cup/35 g rice flour

## DAY 1

Combine the hard red winter wheat flour with ¾ cup/ 190 g of water in the bowl of a stand mixer. Use your hands to mix the flour and water, cover the bowl with plastic wrap, and allow it to sit overnight.

## DAY 2

Add the coarse rye starter, breaking it up with your hands as you add it, along with the fresh cake yeast.

Mix on low with a bread hook until the dough just comes together, about 1 minute. Let the dough rest in the bowl for 30 minutes at room temperature, then add the salt and mix on medium high until the dough comes together tightly around the hook, about 7 minutes.

Transfer the dough to an oiled, medium metal mixing bowl and refrigerate for 20 minutes.

Remove the dough from the refrigerator, wet your hands, and, with the dough still in the bowl, fold it two thirds of the way over itself 4 times, giving it a quarter turn after each fold. Turn the dough over in the bowl, flipping it so the seams in the dough are at the bottom of the bowl. Wait 20 minutes and repeat the 4 folds, cover the bowl with plastic wrap, and refrigerate overnight.

## DAY 3

Preheat the oven with a baking stone set inside to 500°F/260°C. Combine the rye and rice flours and use them to dust a dough-rising basket.

Dust the counter with the same flour and transfer the cool dough to the counter, gently coaxing it from the bowl with a plastic dough card or your hand.

In as few movements as possible, shape the dough into a ball on the counter, taking care not to tear it. The dough should be about 6 inches/15 cm across.

Flip the dough over onto a clean, floured surface and gently form the dough into a ball by giving it about 4 quick quarter turns with cupped hands. Flip the dough one more time, then place it into the dough-rising basket and cover it with a plastic bag or lightly moistened towel. Proof the dough at about 70°F/21°C.

After 40 minutes, poke about ½ inch/1 cm into the dough with a floured finger. It will be ready to bake when the surface of the dough springs back slowly and leaves a slight indent. If it springs back quickly and returns to its original shape, cover and check again in 10 minutes.

Dust a pizza peel with the rice/rye flour mixture. Transfer the loaf from the dough-rising basket to the paddle and slide it into the oven, quickly spraying the surface of the dough and the inside of the oven with a mister.

Bake for 20 minutes, then rotate the loaf 180 degrees and return to the oven for another 20 minutes. Rotate 180 degrees again and return to the oven for another 20 minutes. Test the bread to see if it is done; it should be dark golden brown with a firm bottom that makes a hollow sound when tapped.

Cool the loaf on a wire rack for 30 minutes before slicing.

# CHICKEN DRIPPINGS

4 whole chickens

½ cup/110 g high-quality unsalted butter, plus more for
serving

2 tablespoons/15 g finely diced shallot

2 teaspoons/25 g minced fresh parsley

2 teaspoons/25 g minced fresh tarragon

2 teaspoons/25 g minced fresh chervil

High-quality cider vinegar

Place 3 of the chickens in a stockpot, add water until they're just covered, bring to a boil, and keep them at a low simmer for 4 hours. Strain the liquid through a fine-mesh sieve and discard the carcasses.

Preheat the oven to 400°F/204°C. Rub the remaining chicken all over with the butter, including under the skin and in the cavity. Set it in a roasting pan and roast until it is caramelized and the butter in the pan has browned, about 10 minutes.

Strain the buttery chicken drippings and reserve.

Add the roasted chicken to the strained stock in a large saucepan and bring to a rolling boil. Allow it to reduce, occasionally skimming the foam from the surface, until only a few cups of liquid remain (a couple of hours). Lower the heat to medium to slow the reduction and continue to reduce until the liquid is thick enough to coat a spoon and tastes like you've scooped it up from underneath a perfect roast chicken. There should be about 2 cups.

Pour the liquid through a fine-mesh strainer and stir in the reserved buttery chicken drippings. Stir in the shallots, parsley, tarragon, and chervil. Season with cider vinegar. Pour the liquid into a dipping bowl and serve with a loaf of fresh bread and some good butter.

# TINY SQUID AND CHARRED RADICCHIO WITH GREEN ONIONS

The delicious flavor of bitter vegetables with a deep char is something I try to have on the menu in some form or another most of the year, and I usually use something like frisée, radicchio, endive, escarole, puntarelle, or chicory.

This particular dish came about when we noticed how closely the hue and color pattern of charred radicchio resembles that of caramelized squid. I like to camouflage the purple-red bodies of the squid in a stack of grilled radicchio leaves and drizzle some of the squids' juices over the top. Each uniform-looking bite is full of both roasted and bitter flavors and different textures, accentuated by the sweet squid.

Making the sauce is ingredient- and labor-intensive, and it yields a scant amount, but the result has a great intensity that's worth the effort. The same method works well with razor clams, hearty cuts of meat, and mushrooms.

SERVES 4

16 Puget Sound squid (about 1.4 kg)

Grapeseed oil

Elderberry caper brine (page 241)

½ small head radicchio (about 150 g)

Flake salt

4 teaspoons/40 g charred scallion purée (page 249)

Clean the squid carefully, trying not to tear the skin, and blot it dry with paper towels, reserving 8 of the best mantles on a paper towel–lined tray over ice. Place the remaining mantles and all of the tentacles in a strainer over a bowl—these will be used for stock.

## SQUID STOCK

Pour a thin layer of grapeseed oil into a large sauté pan over medium-high heat. When the oil begins to smoke, work in batches to sauté the stock squid until rosy and beginning to caramelize and release juices, about 45 seconds. After each batch, place the squid and the pan juices in a medium mixing bowl and allow the sauté pan to come back up to temperature, adding more grapeseed oil to the pan, if necessary. When the last batch is done, tightly cover the bowl of cooked squid with plastic wrap and set it in a warm spot for 5 to 10 minutes to allow the squid to release additional juices. Strain the juice into a bowl, pressing down on the squid with the back of a spoon to extract as much liquid as possible, then season with elderberry caper brine.

## RADICCHIO

Peel 2 unblemished leaves from the outside of the radicchio and remove and discard any white sections from them. Tear those leaves into irregular-shaped pieces no larger than ¾ inch/2 cm across and place them in an ice bath for a few minutes to crisp them. Spin the pieces dry in a salad spinner and refrigerate until serving.

Cut the radicchio half in half, pole to pole, leaving 2 quarters. Place a large sauté pan over high heat. Add a layer of grapeseed oil and heat until smoking. Caramelize the flat sides of the radicchio quarters, then test the interior; the radicchio is done when the outer leaves are beginning to wilt, while the interior still maintains some crunch. If it needs more time, return it to the pan, cooking it on its curved exterior surface. Set the radicchio on a tray lined with paper towel and sprinkle it lightly with flake salt.

## TO SERVE

Wipe out the sauté pan with a paper towel, return the pan to high heat, and pour in a thin film of grapeseed oil. Once smoking, sauté the reserved raw squid mantles, dark-side down, holding them flat against the pan with an offset spatula. Sear until almost cooked through and starting to caramelize, 30 to 35 seconds. Flip and cook the squid for a few more seconds, then set it on the paper towel next to the radicchio.

Cut the mantles in half lengthwise, then cut into irregular-shaped pieces about 1¼ x ¾ inch/3 x 2 cm. Remove the core from the cooked radicchio wedges. Tear out and discard the white centers from the leaves. Tear the red sections of the leaves into pieces no larger than 1½ x 1½ inches/3 x 3 cm.

Warm the squid stock in a small saucepan. Combine the squid and torn radicchio in a bowl and toss with a generous tablespoon of squid stock.

Place a scant teaspoon of scallion purée in the center of each serving plate and cover with about 6 pieces of cooked radicchio—folded to give the dish a bit of height—followed by 4 pieces of squid, then 3 pieces of raw radicchio. Drizzle with a bit of the stock and dust each serving with flake salt.

# A FLAVORFUL BROTH OF MATSUTAKE MUSHROOMS
## WITH **YELLOW FOOT CHANTERELLES**

Walking along the shores of Lummi Island, you can see the San Juan archipelago to the west and the Cascade Mountains to the east. There are no sidewalks on Lummi, and the twenty-five-mile-per-hour speed limit is observed with a consistency surprising for a place with no police presence.

In the fall, the best walking is in the forest after the first cold rains of the season. Everyone in the kitchen heads into the woods to look for mushrooms. The forest in the autumn has a unique charm, with a low, gray light, the browns and yellows of fallen leaves, the deep greens of conifers, the earthy smells of leaf decay, and the damp forest duff.

This dish attempts to reflect the earthiness and delicacy of that forest scene. Steaming the yellow foot mushrooms gives them a perfect al dente texture. The matsutake produces a broth that is both bold and delicate and pairs well with the musky yellow foot chanterelles.

SERVES 4

**FOR THE MATSUTAKE STOCK**

5 ounces/150 g matsutake mushrooms, cut into $\frac{1}{4}$-inch-/
    .5 cm-thick slices

Salt

Verjus

**FOR THE STEAMED YELLOW FOOT CHANTERELLES**

5 ounces/150 g yellow foot chanterelles

1 teaspoon/5 g high-quality unsalted butter

Salt

## MATSUTAKE STOCK

Heat a water bath to 185°F/85°C. Place the matsutakes in a sous vide bag, vacuum seal them on high, and cook them at least 6 hours (we let them go overnight) in the water bath. Pour the stock this creates directly from the bag through a fine-mesh sieve and into a small saucepan, using the back of a spoon to press the mushrooms against the strainer wall to extract more stock. Season the stock with salt and verjus and discard the mushrooms.

## STEAMED YELLOW FOOT CHANTERELLES

Wipe the yellow foot chanterelles clean with a damp paper towel, cut out any discolored parts, and trim the stems to about 2 inches/5 cm.

Place the butter, followed immediately by the yellow foot chanterelles, in a small risotto pan over medium heat and season lightly with salt. Stir and toss them constantly to keep them from browning, adding a few drops of water to the pan to kick-start the steaming process, if necessary. Remove them from the heat when they're softened but still firm enough to stand on their caps (think: al dente) and season with salt if needed.

## TO SERVE

Warm the stock in the saucepan. Arrange 8 to 12 yellow foot chanterelles, caps down, in each small, warmed serving bowl. Spoon about 1½ tablespoons of matsutake stock into each bowl.

# FLAX SEED CARAMELS

The first year that I worked at the Inn, we had to do some major cleaning before we could close for the winter. The place was a mess: there was a family of wild cats that lived in the basement dry storage, along with about a dozen old couches and who knows what else. Raquel and I tore out some nasty carpets, and while cleaning out one of the old storage rooms, we found a very old Willows Inn recipe binder that has entries from many chefs dating back to the 1960s. The binder contains some really good recipes that, in some ways, mirror the food we serve here today and the constraints of living on an island. I took finding it as a sign and a challenge to see if I could serve any of the old classics. One of my favorite of these recipes is for flax caramels.

I don't really like to have a bunch of sweets at the end of a full tasting menu. Lots of nice restaurants follow a beautiful dinner with a full array of desserts, and I usually can't help trying them all but wind up regretting it. We have been serving this simple bite at the end of our menu for some time. It's exactly what I would want to close a meal after a few interesting, light desserts.

When you make the rye bread recipe in this book, you end up with lots of toasted flax left on the baking tray. After tasting how good they are, I learned that it is important to steam flax seeds first, then toast them to give them a better texture. This recipe is trickier than it might seem. To get the perfect texture, we have to make it daily and it has to be chock-full of well-toasted flax seeds, but it's such a nice way to punctuate a meal that it's worth the effort.

## YIELDS MORE THAN 100 CUBES

Scant 2 cups/385 g granulated sugar

1 cup firmly packed/200 g dark brown sugar

1 cup/205 g light corn syrup

1 cup plus 2½ tablespoons/225 g flax seed oil

2 cups plus 2 tablespoons/500 g very fresh heavy cream

¾ cup/185 g evaporated milk

2 cups/660 g flax seeds

Heat the sugars, corn syrup, flax seed oil, cream, and evaporated milk in a medium saucepan over medium heat and bring it up to 230°F/110°C, whisking every 10 to 15 minutes. Reduce the heat to low and continue heating until the temperature comes up to 242.5°F/117°C.

Preheat the oven to 350°F/175°C. Mix the flax seeds with ¼ cup/60 g water, spread them across a quarter-sheet pan lined with a Silpat mat (it's best not to use parchment paper here), and bake until crisp and darker in color, about 30 minutes. Remove the seeds from the pan, returning about 2 tablespoons/15 g to the Silpat mat lining the pan and spreading them out evenly.

Reserve about ¼ cup plus 2 tablespoons toasted flax seed. Working quickly, whisk the remaining toasted flax into the caramel, then pour the mixture onto the seed-lined sheet pan. Sprinkle the reserved flax seeds evenly across the top. Allow the caramel to cool to room temperature, then wrap the pan tightly with plastic wrap and refrigerate until it sets.

## TO SERVE

Pull the caramel out of the refrigerator. Allow it to sit at room temperature for 30 minutes before popping it out of the pan and cutting it into ¾-inch/2 cm cubes.

# RIPE PEARS BURIED IN HOT EMBERS

love to work outside, chopping wood next to the smokehouse with a view of the ocean. First thing each morning, we light a huge fire to create embers that we grill with all day long. We use fire for several techniques, bringing in various types of wood from different parts of the island, such as fruit trees, hardwoods, pines, and junipers—each making a significant impact on the finished dish.

It's not uncommon for every dish on the menu to be prepared in some way over fire. We are constantly stacking and rotating firewood around the property: cutting a few trees down at the farm, letting the wood dry over the summer, placing it under cover for the winter, and burning it the following year. However, green alder, the wood that we use for smoking, has to be used almost as soon as the tree is felled. In addition, the bark can only be scraped off just before it goes onto the fire for the right flavors to come through in the food. This means that we are constantly cutting down a few trees or some big branches to keep the smoker going.

When we get a new ingredient, we like to cook it in as many ways as possible to learn how it might taste best. Tossing the whole thing into the embers is always one of the experiments. The super-high direct heat usually creates a hard black carbon shell while the interior steams in its caramelized juices, concentrating the flavor. This method brings out sweetness that roasting does not and a deep-roasted flavor that grilling alone misses. Pears are fantastic when cooked this way, which creates an eggshell-like exterior around a dark-brown, shrunken fruit. We further the flavor by covering the pears with verbena branches just as they finish grilling to perfume their flesh.

SERVES 4

3 ripe Anjou pears (about 75 g)

6 verbena branches (about 250 g)

2 tablespoons/5 g dried woodruff leaves

Verjus

Stock syrup (page 256)

Woodruff oil (page 242)

4 woodruff tips

Build a roaring outdoor fire. Once it's burning hot, nestle the pears in the center of the fire, moving the logs to enclose them without crushing them. When the pears are entirely black with fissures as wide as a pencil, throw the verbena branches on top of them; once the branches are burnt, remove the pears from the fire. Allow them to cool at room temperature.

Preheat the oven to 350°F/175°C. Once the pears are cool enough to handle, coax them out of their charred skin with your hands and discard the skin. Make 2 vertical cuts on either side of the stem of 2 of the pears, avoiding any seed or stem, and leaving you with 2 large pieces of pear per fruit.

Place the pear pieces flat-side down on a parchment-lined half-sheet pan and set the tray aside until serving.

## PEAR-WOODRUFF JUICE

Run the remaining whole pear and pear scraps, cores included, through a juicer. Combine the pear juice and dried woodruff in a small saucepan, bring to a light simmer, then pull the pan off the heat and allow it to steep for 10 minutes. Strain the juice through a Superbag. Season the juice with a few drops of verjus and stock syrup.

## TO SERVE

Put 1 pear slice in each serving bowl, flat-side down. Pour about 1½ tablespoons of the pear-woodruff juice over the top, followed by about 8 drops of woodruff oil on the juice. Garnish with a woodruff tip.

# SLICES OF CELERIAC STEAMED IN BUTTERMILK WITH **FRESH HAZELNUT**

Hazelnuts are a significant fall crop on Lummi, becoming available toward the end of October. Like other nuts, they are easily stored and transported, but only once they've been dried. The real advantage that Lummi's hazelnut harvest gives us is access to the fresh, undried nuts, which have a woody flavor and soft yet crunchy texture that's quite different from the dried nuts.

This is a delicate dish that highlights the subtle flavors of celeriac and fresh hazelnuts, and the final product features flavors that are light but full.

SERVES 4

3 cups/735 g cultured buttermilk

Salt

24 fresh hazelnuts in their shells (about 125 g)

1 medium celeriac (about 130 g)

4 ounces/100 g fresh horseradish root, peeled

Flake salt

Grapeseed oil

Scald the buttermilk by bringing it to the edge of boiling in a saucepan over medium-high heat. Let it cool for a few minutes, then pass it through a fine-mesh strainer to remove the solids from the whey. Discard the solids and season the whey with salt.

Shell the hazelnuts (we do this by folding a nut inside a dish towel and cracking it with a small saucepan) and put them in a medium bowl. Cover them with boiling water, wait 2 minutes, then use a paring knife to peel off their skins. Use a mandoline to create 1⁄16-inch-/2 mm-thick lengthwise slices of hazelnut and place the slices in an ice bath for about 5 minutes to crisp them. Remove the slices from the water and store them in a container lined with a moist paper towel until serving.

Peel the celeriac and cut 4 cross sections about 1⁄4 inch/.5 cm thick out of the center. Lay the slices in a single layer on the bottom of a saucepan or sauté pan just large enough to accommodate them. Pour in the buttermilk whey until it comes about halfway up their sides and lay a circle of parchment paper cut to fit inside the pan directly on the celeriac and whey. Set the saucepan over medium-low heat until the whey begins to bubble, then adjust the heat to maintain a low simmer. Remove the pan from the heat when the celeriac is just tender enough to cut easily with a dinner knife.

## TO SERVE

Set a warm celeriac slice at the center of each serving bowl. Pour 2 teaspoons of whey from the saucepan over the top, followed by about 8 horseradish ribbons (about 1 inch/2.5 cm long) made by scraping a knife edge down the length of the root. Sprinkle the top of the celeriac with a pinch of flake salt, then lay hazelnut slices across it, allowing them to overlap a bit and cover the celeriac completely. Spoon about a teaspoon of grapeseed oil over the hazelnut slices.

# KALE CHIPS

I like to serve these chips along with a very good local cider before the meal begins. I love their crunchy texture and earthy flavor. They are best made from fall or winter Lacinato kale leaves, which are thicker and sturdier than the spring leaves. We lightly brush them with grapeseed oil and bake them in the oven just before serving, dotting the crisp leaves with a sauce of Olympic Peninsula black truffles and rye breadcrumbs.

SERVES 4

**FOR THE KALE LEAVES**

2 wide leaves Lacinato kale

Grapeseed oil

**FOR THE TRUFFLE EMULSION AND RYE**

1 slice seeded rye bread (page 244)

1 teaspoon/5 g high-quality unsalted butter

4 ounces/100 g Olympic Peninsula black truffles

2 tablespoons plus 1 teaspoon/24 g truffle oil

1 scant tablespoon/12 g chicken drippings (page 191)

Scant ⅓ cup/60 g grapeseed oil

High-quality cider vinegar

Salt

**KALE LEAVES**

Preheat the oven to 350°F/175°C. Tear the kale leaves from their stems and brush them lightly with the grapeseed oil. Roll aluminum foil into 5 batons that are about ½ inch/1 cm wide and 18 inches/45 cm long. Place the leaves on top of 2 of the aluminum foil batons on a sheet pan, then place the 3 remaining batons on top of the leaves to mold them into wave shapes. Bake until the kale is crisp enough to break, about 5 minutes.

**TRUFFLE EMULSION AND RYE**

Roughly chop the rye bread, then pulse it in a food processor to a coarse crumb texture. Heat a medium sauté pan with the butter and toast the rye crumbs until brown and crisp.

Pulse the truffles, truffle oil, and chicken drippings in a blender at high speed until well combined. Slowly pour in the grapeseed oil to create an emulsification that is smooth like mayonnaise. Season to taste with cider vinegar and salt.

**TO SERVE**

Dot the crispy kale leaves with pea-sized dollops of the truffle emulsion, about 8 per leaf, then coat each dollop with rye crumbs.

# LAMB WITH GRASSES

Cooking with meat is a very meaningful process for us because the people who raise the animals that we use do so with great care. I get a chance to visit the farms and the animals that we serve at the Inn. The animals are really more like members of a farmer's family that happen to taste great.

There are many ways that the meat from a great animal can be spoiled. Poor butchery, improper storage, and, of course, bad cooking technique can destroy the quality of a beautifully raised creature, so we take great care at every stage. Aging meats properly is key, and after we receive a carcass, we usually break it down into quarters and hang them for a week before basting the exterior with rendered fat. Most animal flesh needs at least three weeks of hanging before its flavor and texture is at its best. Meat like venison benefits from being hung for at least six to eight weeks.

We get around fifteen lambs a year in the summer or fall, and usually a pig or a cow. We only work with whole animals because we are usually buying from small farms that just have a few animals. The farmers take pride in the quality of every inch of what they have raised.

I like to cook large cuts of meat over the fire or roast whole cuts in a hot oven, let them rest, then portion and serve them immediately. This means that the timing of the cooking during dinner service has to be exact, as some cuts might take several hours to cook.

SERVES 10

1 bone-in pasture-raised lamb leg (about 1.5 kg), aged at least 6 weeks

⅔ cup/70 g kosher salt

**FOR THE MARROW SAUCE**

10 ounces/265 g lamb marrow

1 large shallot (about 85 g), finely chopped

16 salt-cured anchovies, crushed into a paste

**FOR THE WHEATGRASS JUICE**

½ cup/120 g wheatgrass juice

Salt

Verjus

High-quality cider vinegar

2 teaspoons/10 g spinach purée (page 247)

**FOR THE WHEATGRASS EMULSION**

3½ ounces/100 g chopped wheatgrass

1 tablespoon plus 2 teaspoons/25 g wheatgrass juice

1 tablespoon plus 1 teaspoon/20 g high-quality cider vinegar

1 teaspoon/6 g Dijon mustard

⅔ cup/150 g grapeseed oil

Clarified unsalted butter

3 ounces/90 g lamb marrow

1½ ounces/40 g fresh rosemary leaves

1½ ounces/40 g fresh tarragon leaves

3 ounces/80 g wheatgrass, chopped into ½-inch/1 cm pieces

Remove the bone from the leg of lamb and separate the 3 interior muscle groups. Pour 2 quarts/2 L of water into a container with the salt and stir to dissolve. Add the lamb cuts and cover the container with a lid. Let it brine for 3 hours in the refrigerator. Tie the 3 leg muscles with butcher's twine spaced out about every 1½ inches/4 cm.

## MARROW SAUCE

Render the 10 ounces/265 g of lamb marrow in a saucepan over low heat, 5 to 10 minutes. Strain out any impurities and return the rendered marrow to the saucepan. Add the shallot and anchovies and simmer for 10 minutes, stirring occasionally, to allow the flavors to marry. Keep the sauce warm in the pot until serving.

## WHEATGRASS JUICE

Pour the wheatgrass juice into an immersion blender jar and season it with salt, verjus, and cider vinegar. Add the spinach purée and blend the juice with the immersion blender until incorporated. Set aside for at least 1 hour to settle, then skim any foam from the top.

## WHEATGRASS EMULSION

Combine the chopped wheatgrass, wheatgrass juice, cider vinegar, and Dijon mustard in the blender. Blend on high for 30 seconds, then, with the blender still on high, slowly stream in the grapeseed oil as you would with a mayonnaise. Strain the emulsion through a fine-mesh strainer.

## LAMB

Preheat the oven to 500°F/260°C. Heat a large skillet over high heat. Sear the lamb in clarified butter on both sides to get a dark, caramelized crust. Set the lamb pieces on a rack set over a roasting pan in the oven. Finish the lamb to medium doneness (about 20 minutes), then allow it to rest under foil for 10 minutes.

## TO SERVE

Roughly chop the 3 ounces/90 g of marrow. Off the heat, stir the chopped marrow, rosemary, tarragon, and chopped wheatgrass into the warm marrow sauce.

Remove the twine from the lamb and cut it into ½-inch-/1 cm-thick slices.

Place a teaspoon of the wheatgrass emulsion in the center of each warmed dinner plate and top with a slice of lamb. Finish with a teaspoon of marrow sauce and a teaspoon of wheatgrass juice over the lamb.

# A DESSERT OF QUINCE FRUITS
# THAT GROW AROUND THE KITCHEN

There's a big quince bush in front of the restaurant, and I like to watch it throughout the year. It is one of the earliest plants to bloom on the island, sometimes blossoming as early as February, bursting with edible orange flowers in the spring. There's a long wait before the fruit is ripe in the late fall, and it hangs on into the winter, when the leaves fall from the bush. There are more than ten types of quince that grow on the island. Some ripen to be large and sweet, closer to the size of an apple or pear, others are smaller with large seeds and very tart flesh. I like to use the raw, grated flesh of the smaller ones as a tart seasoning on vegetables or meats, or turn their juice into a vinegar we can use later in the year. For this recipe, we use three types of quince that ripen in the trees around the Inn at different times throughout the fall. Two of them we juice and freeze as a granita, then we wait for the late-season quince out front to ripen before we put this dish on the menu as the first dessert that goes out to the floor.

Once the bush out front is ready, we try to stretch the short season that its fruit are available for as long as possible. We only use three or four of the small fruits per day, and in the past we have managed to keep serving this dish even when we've had to dig through the snow and ice to find the fruit.

SERVES 4

**FOR THE QUINCE GRANITA**

1 cup/235 g pineapple quince juice (about 2 pounds/1 kg quince run through the juicer)

Pinch of ascorbic acid

Verjus

Stock syrup (page 256)

**FOR THE YOGURT MOUSSE**

2 sheets bronze leaf gelatin

2½ fresh egg whites from Riley Starks (about 75 g)

½ cup/125 g heavy whipping cream

Scant ⅓ cup/150 g high-quality plain yogurt, divided

2 tablespoons/25 g granulated sugar

1 teaspoon/5 g verjus, plus more to season

1 small, tart quince (about 10 g)

1 (10-inch/25 cm) square rosemary candy (page 255)

### QUINCE GRANITA

Pour the quince juice into a loaf pan, stir in the ascorbic acid, and season with verjus and stock syrup. (Season with a heavier hand than normal, as the flavors will be less pronounced once this freezes.) Place the pan in the freezer, scraping and stirring with a fork every 10 minutes until completely frozen.

Scrape the surface of the frozen juice in a crosshatch pattern with the tines of a fork to create the granita. Reserve the granita in a pre-frozen container in the freezer.

### YOGURT MOUSSE

Soak the gelatin sheets in a bowl of cold water until they bloom—becoming hydrated and completely supple—5 to 10 minutes. Place the egg whites, heavy cream, and yogurt into their own individual medium metal mixing bowls.

Squeeze the gelatin to remove any excess water and place it in a small saucepan over medium heat. Scoop a few spoonfuls of the yogurt in with the gelatin and stir it with a spatula until it just starts to steam, about 30 seconds. Whisk the mixture into the bowl with the remaining yogurt and allow the contents to cool to room temperature.

Add the granulated sugar to the heavy cream and whisk until stiff peaks form.

Fold the whipped cream into the yogurt mixture, one whiskful at a time. Continue until the whipped cream is thoroughly incorporated.

Pour the teaspoon/5 g of verjus into the egg whites and whisk until stiff peaks form. Gently fold the beaten whites into the yogurt mixture, one whiskful at a time, switching to a rubber scraper for the last whiskful of whites to keep as much air in the mixture as possible. Season with more verjus, if desired. Transfer the mousse to a piping bag.

### TO SERVE

Grate the quince with a Microplane. Break the rosemary candy into small shards, no larger than 1 x ½ inch/2 x 1 cm.

Pipe about 2 tablespoons of the yogurt mousse into the center of each small serving bowl. Cover the mousse with about ¼ cup of granita. Space out 8 or 9 pea-sized dollops of grated quince on top of the granita. Place about 10 shards of the rosemary candy into the granita, arranged vertically, and sprinkle another pinch of the grated quince over the top.

## TOASTED BREAD, SWEET POTATOES, AND WHIPPED CREAM

I love the texture of roasted sweet potatoes, but I never thought that there could be much more to them until I started to buy their seeds and plant them on the farm. I learned that there are dozens of varieties from around the world. Growing several of them at once and tasting their differences side by side inspired this autumnal dessert. Depending on the potatoes you use, the time of year, and their growing conditions, it might be best to place the roasted potatoes into the dehydrator for a few hours before slicing.

How I make the sweet potato dessert:

Wake up and mill about the house for a few and have some breakfast with Raquel.

Walk to work in the rain and pick up some cress along the way. As I walk up the driveway, I wave to Nick, who is starting the smokehouse fire and lighting the grill. I walk into the kitchen through the back door just in time to get the last of the staff breakfast, some nicely scrambled eggs and toast with jam. I double-check yesterday's menu selections against the updated reservations sheet, post a copy in the kitchen, and give one to each chef. We have a few more chefs now than we once did, so I usually pick up where I left off from yesterday's projects, taking a moment to make sure that the bread is being mixed and the bread oven is heating. I check in with Nick about any product issues or new ideas, and he mentions that the beach mustard is beginning to seed and that they taste amazing after a strong rain. I taste the spruce-infused cream from the night before and add a few fresh spruce branches to it, then toast some bread and nuts in the oven and pick and blacken some bay leaves for the crumble. Mary the farmer comes by with an unscheduled delivery—a few odds and ends from the garden—and to say hi. The kitchen is busy during the day, and there is rarely a time when there is any open space on the stove or in the oven. We listen to a Wayne album or two. Nick usually has a few new dishes he's working on that we taste and develop during the day, and we both help out where needed. I notice that the oven is close to temp and seal the door for the temperature to equalize for a few hours. I make a call to Jean that we would like more goat milk for tomorrow, and I get a text from Jeremy the fisherman saying he will be a day late coming to shore. I work on coming up with a new eggplant dish to take advantage of the surplus of beautiful eggplants at the farm. At some point, I move off the pass where I usually prep so that the bread can be portioned and hear the thumping of a tugboat passing between Lummi and Orcas Island. I prepare the sweet potatoes to be roasted during service and make a quick meringue. Raquel arrives in the afternoon and starts to set up the dining room while the rest of the team trickles in, and before long our tiny kitchen is crowded with chefs and the waitstaff. I pick down some spruce tips as each chef brings over the dish they're responsible for, allowing us to ensure that each dish tastes just right before service begins. At four, we have a staff meeting around the pass to go over the evening's menu, noting any returning guests, dietary restrictions, and new dishes. Just before service, I make sure the oven is set to 350°F/175°C. Much later in the evening, we roast and peel the sweet potatoes, slicing them into coin-shaped pieces while we whip the spruce-infused cream and toast dollops of meringue on the plates.

After the desserts are made, most of the chefs head to the dining room to talk with guests while Trevor collects a few spruce branches that will be used with tomorrow's cream, then we start scrubbing down the kitchen.

## FOR THE SPRUCE WHIPPED CREAM

1 cup/225 g very fresh heavy whipping cream

1 cup/30 g small, tender northern spruce tips

¾ tablespoon/10 g granulated sugar

## FOR THE SWEET POTATOES

3 small sweet potatoes (about 250 g)

2 tablespoons/30 g clarified high-quality unsalted butter

## FOR THE BAY LEAF CRUMBLE

½ cup/75 g skin-on raw hazelnuts

½ cup/75 g blanched almonds

½ cup/75 g pine nuts

½ cup/75 g pecans

¼ cup plus 2 teaspoons firmly packed/60 g dark brown sugar, divided

4 tablespoons/60 g melted high-quality unsalted butter, divided

2 slices pain de mie (1 inch/2.5 cm thick)

15 fresh bay leaves

4 tablespoons meringue (page 255)

20 tender northern spruce tips

## SPRUCE WHIPPED CREAM

A day ahead, combine the heavy cream and the cup/30 g of spruce tips. Cover and refrigerate overnight.

## SWEET POTATOES

Preheat the oven to 350°F/175°C. Bake the sweet potatoes until just cooked through, about 20 minutes. Allow the potatoes to cool, then peel and cut them into ⅛-inch-/3 mm-thick slices. Brush them with the clarified butter and set aside. Leave the oven at 350°F/175°C for the crumble.

## BAY LEAF CRUMBLE

Cut the hazelnuts and almonds in half lengthwise, then combine them with the pine nuts and pecans in a metal mixing bowl. Add half of the brown sugar and half of the melted butter to the bowl and stir to coat the nuts. Spread the nuts evenly across a Silpat mat or parchment-lined baking sheet. Place the nuts in the oven until they are lightly browned, about 15 minutes. Allow the nuts to cool, then roughly chop them.

While the nuts are cooking, remove and discard the crust from the pain de mie slices. Tear the bread into dime-sized pieces and place them on a Silpat mat or parchment-lined baking sheet, then put them in the oven next to the nuts until crisp but not browned.

Place the remaining brown sugar and remaining melted butter in a mixing bowl with the toasted bread. Toss until the bread is coated, then return to the oven on the Silpat/parchment-lined baking sheet until the crumbs are a nice golden brown, 5 to 10 minutes longer. Stir them into the nut mixture.

Toast all but 2 of the bay leaves in a large skillet over high heat, flipping once and removing them from the heat when they release their aroma and are just starting to brown around the edges, about 30 seconds. Remove and discard the stems from all of the fresh and toasted bay leaves. Roughly chop all of the leaves and run them through a spice grinder until they have an almost powderlike consistency.

## SPRUCE WHIPPED CREAM

Remove the spruce tip and cream mixture from the refrigerator and strain it through a fine-mesh sieve into a medium metal mixing bowl, using a wooden spoon to push out as much liquid as possible. Add the granulated sugar to the bowl and whip the cream until soft peaks form.

## TO SERVE

Place a tablespoon-sized dollop of meringue near the edge of each small serving plate, smear it across the plate with the back of a spoon, then toast some of the exterior with a blowtorch. Sprinkle a tablespoon of the bay leaf crumble on top of the meringue, followed by 3 slices of sweet potato. Spoon a dollop of the whipped cream onto the plate and garnish it with 5 fresh spruce tips.

# A CONFITURE OF WILD MUSHROOMS
## AND *FRESHLY PICKED JUNIPER BERRIES*

When the fall rains come, the island erupts with mushrooms of every type. Even if it's a sign of cooler, damper weather ahead, it's impossible not to look forward to their arrival when they can grow so thick that they can carpet the forest floor.

Raquel and I like to walk through the woods just to look at the different types of mushrooms and the strange places they appear. We find neon-orange jelly mushrooms, specimens that have grown like a great coral reef, and giants that pop up overnight. The different colors and endless shapes and textures can look like something from a science fiction movie.

This dish is served at the height of mushroom season, when we have dozens of wild mushrooms available. During the day, I like to gently cook them in fat: we poach each variety individually in butter with a few herbs to preserve their unique shapes, colors, and flavors. We hold the mushrooms in the fat for a few hours after cooking and serve them at room temperature. When it's time to serve, we paint the bowl with a juniper berry purée that mimics the aroma of the forest floor.

SERVES 4

**FOR THE MUSHROOMS**

5 ounces/150 g mixed fall forest mushrooms, such as chanterelle, matsutake, porcini, saffron milk cap, and lobster, cleaned and trimmed

1½ cups/365 g grapeseed oil

1½ cups/340 g clarified high-quality unsalted butter

1 fresh bay leaf

1 sprig thyme

**FOR THE BREAD**

1 slice pain de mie

1 teaspoon/5 g high-quality unsalted butter

1 teaspoon/5 g grapeseed oil

**FOR THE JUNIPER PURÉE**

⅓ cup/80 g spinach purée (page 247)

⅓ cup/80 g Juniper oil (page 242)

¼ cup/60 g juniper vinegar (page 130)

1 tablespoon/12 g Stock syrup (page 256)

Salt

1½ teaspoons/5 g Fermented green garlic brine (page 240)

1 cup/240 g mushroom stock (page 250)

Flake salt

**FOR SERVING**

4 teaspoons/15 g elderberry capers (page 241)

20 rosette cress leaves

## MUSHROOMS

Set aside the 2 best sturdy and thick-stemmed chanterelle mushrooms and cut all the remaining mushrooms into pieces slightly larger than bite-size—this will highlight the shape and size of each mushroom in the finished dish. Keep the varieties separate from one another.

Combine the grapeseed oil and clarified butter in a medium saucepan over low heat to make the mushroom poaching fat and bring it up to 170°F/77°C.

Add the bay leaf and thyme to the saucepan. Cook each variety of mushroom (except the chanterelles that have been set aside) in the fat separately, each batch covered with 2 sheets of parchment paper cut to fit directly on the surface of the mushrooms and melted fat. Remove each variety when just cooked through and place them on a paper towel–lined sheet pan. Once all of the mushrooms are cooked, combine them in the fat and reserve until serving, off the heat.

## BREAD

Cut off and discard the crust from the pain de mie and tear into 4 bite-sized pieces. Place a medium sauté pan over medium heat and add the butter and grapeseed oil. Once the butter has foamed, add the bread pieces, turning occasionally, cooking them until just golden, 3 to 5 minutes.

## JUNIPER PURÉE

Place the spinach purée in a medium bowl and whisk in the juniper oil, adding it in a thin stream. Incorporate the juniper vinegar, then the stock syrup. Season the mixture with salt and the green garlic brine.

## TO SERVE

Preheat the oven to 350°F/175°C.

Gently combine the mushroom stock and ¼ cup/60 g of the fat used to cook the mushrooms in a small saucepan, giving it a stir with a spoon. (We're going for the effect of drops of one floating on the other, not an emulsification.) Keep the mixture warm in the saucepan over very low heat.

Use a mandoline to create paper-thin vertical slices of the reserved raw mushrooms, about 4 slices of each mushroom per dish.

Drain the cooked mushrooms in a fine-mesh sieve and allow them to continue to drain for a minute. Lightly dress the cooked mushrooms with the juniper purée.

Place one of each type of cooked mushroom in each serving bowl, along with a piece of the bread. Sprinkle the cooked mushrooms with a teaspoon of elderberry capers, a few slices of the raw mushrooms, and 5 rosette cress leaves. Spoon a tablespoon of the mushroom stock and fat mixture into the bottom of the bowl.

# PRESERVED ROSE HIPS WITH **WARM MILK JAM**

The island's north coast is lined with wild Nootka roses, which grow so thickly that they can form a near-impenetrable barrier, impeding access to some of our more private beaches. When you pick them in the winter, their deep-red rose hips stand out against the dried bushes around them, some of the only bright colors in the winter wilderness.

For most people, rose hips are an unfamiliar ingredient, perhaps recognizable only from their inclusion in some herbal tea blends or vitamin supplements. Turning them into a main ingredient was a challenge that took some trial and error. A large amount of the fruit is inedible, consisting mostly of a tough, fibrous core.

This method of turning the rose hips into ice cream results in something vibrant and several degrees brighter and more intense than the raw rose hips themselves. It's a great way to give guests a blast of fruit flavor during a season when they might expect something darker or earthier.

SERVES 4

### FOR THE ROSE HIP ICE CREAM

25 ounces/750 g fresh, whole rose hip berries, stemmed

½ teaspoon/2.5 g citric acid

⅔ cup/140 g granulated sugar

⅓ cup plus 1 tablespoon/100 g Stock syrup (page 256)

3 tablespoons plus 2 teaspoons/55 g rhubarb wine (page 237)

3 tablespoons plus 1 teaspoon/50 g elderflower syrup

### FOR THE CRUSHED ROSE HIPS

20 fresh, large rose hip berries

Verjus

### FOR THE MILK JAM

1 quart/1 L very fresh whole milk

½ cup/100 g very fresh heavy cream

½ cup/100 g granulated sugar

## ROSE HIP ICE CREAM

Mix the whole rose hips, citric acid, granulated sugar, stock syrup, rhubarb wine, and elderflower syrup together in a medium saucepan. Cover the pan and allow the ingredients to macerate overnight in the refrigerator.

The next morning, add ⅔ cup/140 g of water to the pan, cover it with plastic wrap, and simmer until the berries are tender but still brightly colored, about 90 minutes.

Pass the mixture through a food mill into a medium saucepan and add another ⅔ cup/140 g of water. Push the mixture through a medium-fine sieve and into a mixing bowl.

Divide the mixture between 2 Pacojet beakers and freeze them overnight.

## CRUSHED ROSE HIPS

Halve all of the rose hips, pole to pole, scoop out and discard the seeds and pith, and crush the skins with the back of a spoon in a small bowl, while leaving the halves intact. Season with a few drops of verjus.

## MILK JAM

Combine the milk, heavy cream, and sugar in a medium saucepan over very low heat. Keep it just below a simmer for about 6 hours, uncovered, stirring occasionally with a wooden spoon, until clumps form and it is significantly thickened, like a loose yogurt.

## TO SERVE

Process the ice cream in the Pacojet. Put a tablespoon of warm milk jam in the bottom of each small serving bowl. Arrange a few crushed rose hips on top of the jam, then, working quickly, set a spoonful of the rose hip ice cream over the top and serve immediately.

# SALT-CURED BONE MARROW WITH BERRIES AND DRIED BEETS

The cool, mild climate of the Pacific Northwest seems to be perfect for growing beets. Mary delivers the first crop as they are harvested from mid-May until late June, and then the second one lasts for a few weeks in mid-fall. Beets store well, so if the yield is sufficient, we can serve beets for most of the year.

We've served beets roasted, salt-baked, pickled, and smoked, but this method is my favorite. For this dish, they are steamed with honey until tender, dehydrated, then rehydrated in a glaze of lingonberry and beet juices. The lingonberries are added toward the end, lending their tart juices to balance out the dish.

On top of the dish, we set coin-sized pieces of warmed beef marrow, the part of the cow where the quality and health of the animal is most apparent. We get our beef bones from Charlie Baker, who pastures his cows on the edge of the uninhabited end of the island. We soak the bones in warm water, saw the ends off, and slide the marrow out in one large piece before shocking it in ice water to firm it back up. The technique we use for salt-curing and drying the bone marrow before a partial rendering is unconventional and is the best way I have found to use bone marrow.

It is amazing what the right herb can do to finish a dish. In this case, the deep flavors of beef and beets are complemented nicely by a few thyme tips and a drizzle of thyme oil.

SERVES 4

**FOR THE MARROW**

1 pound/500 g beef marrow

10 ounces/280 g salt, divided

**FOR THE DEHYDRATED BEETS**

4 large beets (about 900 g)

3 tablespoons plus 2 teaspoons/50 g grapeseed oil

½ cup/150 g honeycomb loaded with honey

3 sprigs thyme

4 fresh bay leaves

1 sprig rosemary

2 sprigs parsley

**FOR THE BEET SAUCE**

10 pounds/4.5 kg beets

**FOR THE TOASTED SEEDS**

1 teaspoon each fennel seeds, dill seeds, mustard seeds, beet seeds, flax seeds, and caraway seeds

**FOR SERVING**

⅓ cup/100 g fresh lingonberry juice

½ cup/100 g fresh lingonberries

High-quality cider vinegar

Thyme oil (page 242)

24 thyme tips

## MARROW

Cure the marrow in a brine of 1 quart/1 L of water with 2½ ounces/70 g of the salt for 48 hours, changing the brine every 12 hours. Remove the marrow from the brine and allow it to dry overnight on a rack set over a parchment-lined half-sheet pan in the refrigerator. Slice the marrow crosswise into 16 rounds that are about ¼ inch/.5 cm thick and keep them in the refrigerator until serving. Roughly chop and render the remaining marrow in a small saucepan over low heat, straining out any solids. Keep the rendered marrow in its saucepan next to the stove.

## DEHYDRATED BEETS

Preheat the oven to 400°F/205°C. Cut the 4 beets into quarters, leaving the skin attached, and toss them in a bowl with the grapeseed oil. Pour about 5 cups/1175 g of water into a half-sheet pan and whisk in the honeycomb, breaking it into small pieces, then add the thyme, bay leaves, rosemary, and parsley. Set a grate in the sheet pan and put the beets on it. Cover the pan with plastic wrap, then aluminum foil, and cook until the beets are slightly overcooked (they'll feel a bit waterlogged), about 2 hours.

Allow the beets to cool, then peel off the skin and lay them out in a single layer on a dehydrator tray. Set the dehydrator to 90°F/32°C and dry the beets until their edges are almost crisp (they'll have a texture like a raisin or a prune), about 5 hours.

## BEET SAUCE

Run the 10 pounds/4.5 kg of beets through the juicer, stopping once you've got 1 quart/1 L of juice. Put the juice in a saucepan, bring to a simmer, and allow it to bubble away until it's a thick syrup that's a tenth of its original volume (a little more than ⅓ cup/100 g). Keep an eye on the edge of the liquid as it reduces and change pans if you get a ring of caramelizing juice around the edges—this will burn and impart an off taste.

## TOASTED SEEDS

Toast all of the seeds together in a sauté pan over medium heat until they perfume the air with their aroma. Set aside until serving.

## TO SERVE

Warm the pan with the rendered marrow over low heat. Warm the rounds of cured marrow in a small sauté pan over low heat until they have the first signs of translucence, about 30 seconds. Heat the dehydrated beets with the beet sauce and the lingonberry juice in a small saucepan over low heat, allowing the dehydrated beets to glaze and soak up some of the liquid, about 5 minutes. Stir in about a tablespoon of the warm rendered marrow and the fresh lingonberries and season the mixture with cider vinegar, if necessary, to balance the sweetness and acidity.

Divide the beets and fresh lingonberries between each serving plate, top with 4 slices of the cured marrow, drizzle with a teaspoon of thyme oil, sprinkle with a teaspoon of the toasted seeds, and garnish with the thyme tips.

# A DESSERT OF FRESH CHESTNUTS AND GREEN HAZELNUTS

Cooking with fresh nuts is an incredible process. I like shaving the sharp spikes from the hard skin of a chestnut, followed by the cracking, blanching, peeling, and roasting. It makes nuts seem like a real treasure, not just something that comes in a plastic bag.

This recipe—a fluffy and tacky purée of chestnuts served hot next to a smooth scoop of green hazelnut ice cream— pairs the two freshly harvested nuts in a dish that can be made for a month or so in the fall.

SERVES 4

### FOR THE HAZELNUT ICE CREAM

18 ounces/500 g fresh hazelnuts, blanched

½ cup/100 g granulated sugar

¼ cup plus 1 tablespoon/50 g milk powder

4¼ cups/1 L very fresh whole milk

¼ cup/43 g corn syrup

½ cup/120 g very fresh heavy whipping cream

Pinch of/1 g xanthan gum

3 tablespoons/24 g roasted hazelnut oil

### FOR THE CHESTNUT PURÉE

15 fresh, shell-on chestnuts (about 300 g)

Salt

Stock syrup (page 256)

### FOR SERVING

Roasted hazelnut oil

Flake salt

## HAZELNUT ICE CREAM

Preheat the oven to 275°F/135°C. Toast the blanched hazelnuts on a half-sheet pan in the oven until they are aromatic but not browning, about 15 minutes.

Combine the granulated sugar, milk powder, whole milk, and corn syrup in a medium saucepan and bring to a simmer over low heat, stirring occasionally. Add the cream and return to a simmer, then stir in the xanthan gum.

Pour the milk mixture and the 3 tablespoons/24 g hazelnut oil into a blender. Add the toasted hazelnuts and blend on high until liquefied, about 30 seconds. Carefully open the lid of the blender enough to let steam escape. Let the mixture sit overnight in the refrigerator, then strain it through a Superbag into 2 Pacojet beakers, stopping a few tablespoons' worth of space below the fill line. Discard the solids and put the beakers in the freezer.

## CHESTNUT PURÉE

Bring a large saucepan of water to a boil, add the chestnuts, and simmer for 6 minutes. Remove the pan from the heat, leave the chestnuts in the water, and begin peeling them immediately, removing the entire shell and all of the inner skin underneath.

Half fill a stockpot with water and bring it to a boil. Vacuum seal the cooked chestnuts in a sous vide bag with a few tablespoons of water (there should be just enough water to keep the bag air-free when vacuum sealed). Place the bag in the stockpot with the boiling water and simmer until the chestnuts are completely tender, about an hour.

Blend the cooked chestnuts and their liquid on low in a heavy-duty blender, adding just enough hot water to get the blades to catch, then work the blender up to high, frequently scraping down the insides of the blender. Blend like this for several minutes (the blender and the nuts will get hot), until the chestnuts become completely smooth and slightly aerated. Push the paste through a strainer with a spatula and season with salt and stock syrup.

## TO SERVE

Put each small serving bowl in the freezer. Pour about a tablespoon of roasted hazelnut oil on top of each full beaker of frozen ice cream and run the Pacojet, processing the whole beaker at once to incorporate the oil.

Heat the chestnut purée in a small saucepan over low heat, constantly stirring and scraping down the sides of the pan until it is hot throughout. Working quickly, use 2 spoons to create a 2-bite quenelle of ice cream for each bowl, next to a quenelle of the chestnut purée. (Less ice cream will melt if you put the ice cream in the bowls first.) Drizzle some roasted hazelnut oil between the quenelles and put a flake or two of flake salt on the ice cream.

# WILD VENISON LEG CURED OVER WINTER

In the late fall, I bury a few wild venison legs in salt and herbs for two weeks, stacking them as you might for prosciutto to push the salt all the way to the bone. I then hang the legs up high in the smokehouse for the next two weeks, where they get gently smoked along with the salmon during the day, then cool in the nighttime air. We close for the winter from December until March, and before I lock up for the season, I hang the legs in the cellar beneath the dining room to dry until spring. In March, when I return to the kitchen, they are about a third of their original size, firm, and dark. The whole cellar smells like deer. Slicing into the leg reveals a deep-red interior with a creamy texture and a nice smoky flavor throughout, and I serve a few shavings of it with cocktails before dinner.

YIELDS 2 LEGS

460 g flake salt
230 g granulated sugar
115 g juniper berries
230 g tender pine tips
2 legs from a freshly killed deer (about 6 kg each),
    aged 4 weeks

Mix the salt, sugar, juniper berries, and pine tips together and coat the venison with the mixture, using your hands to massage it into the legs. Place the legs on top of each other in a container just large enough for them. Refrigerate the legs for 2 weeks, flipping the legs over and switching top for bottom once a day.

Rinse off the legs and hang them in the top of a smoker. Keep the legs in the smoker for 2 weeks, smoking with smoldering alderwood 8 hours a day. Move the legs to a dry, cool cellar and hang them there for 2 months.

# HOW TO MAKE **DANDELION VINEGAR**

Seasoning is probably the most important step in any recipe, subtly making food taste better than you think it could. We have a whole cupboard of homemade seasonings that add new dimensions to each dish on the menu. Sometimes, it's the brine from capered elderberries that gives a jus from roasted squid a full and balanced flavor, other times a drop of plum blossom vinegar or a grating of dried smelt will do the trick. Seasonings help create our identity as a restaurant, our own flavor profile that sets us apart from other restaurants. Try making all of the base recipes here, and hopefully a few types of each: they are great tools to make your food taste even better.

Vinegar is a great example. We make many types of it throughout the year. In some cases, we take an ingredient that is full of flavor but can have a terrible texture, like dandelions, and turn it into a flavorful vinegar. (You could make this simple but very flavorful vinegar after weeding the garden in the spring!) We make vinegars, using more or less the same technique given here, for all types of ingredients throughout the year, allowing us to extend the bright flavor of highly seasonal ingredients for the whole year. We make a small amount of vinegar from almost every fruit blossom, fruit juice, and herb that we use, not always knowing how they might end up contributing to the menu. As you get more experienced and begin to use hard-to-find wild ingredients, try using a refractometer and a hydrometer, which will help measure the sweetness and alcohol level, to produce the best and most consistent results.

YIELDS 1 QUART/1 L

2¼ pounds/1 kg dandelion flowers, stems attached
1¼ cups/250 g granulated sugar
1 teaspoon/2 g Champagne yeast
¼ cup/50 g vinegar mother

Place the dandelion flowers in a nonreactive container and add 1 quart/1 L just-boiled water and the sugar. Once it's cooled to room temperature, add the yeast.

Cover the container with cheesecloth. Leave the container out at room temperature until no longer effervescent, 2 to 3 weeks. Add the vinegar mother, re-cover, and leave exposed to the air until it reaches a vinegar acidity level. Bottle and refrigerate the vinegar.

# HOW TO MAKE **RHUBARB WINE**

During my first fall on Lummi, we split a few huge rhubarb plants into individual starts with a little root attached and planted two long rows of green rhubarb up at Nettles Farm. We ended up with a relentless jungle of rhubarb almost head high, with beach ball–sized leaves, and served the rhubarb a few ways on the menu. But even so, I was not making much of a dent in our harvest. We made jams and froze the juices and still had too much, so we read up on winemaking and have since been making and bottling batches of sparkling rhubarb wine each spring and fall, greeting each new guest with a glass.

YIELDS 4 (750 ML) BOTTLES

10 pounds/4.5 kg green rhubarb, roughly chopped, divided

6¼ cups/1425 g granulated sugar, divided

1 teaspoon/5 g Côte des Blancs yeast

Place half the rhubarb in a blender and blend until liquefied, then strain the juice through a Superbag and discard the solids.

Put the remaining rhubarb in a pressure cooker with 1 quart/1 L of water. Run the pressure cooker on high for an hour, then press the cooked rhubarb through a fine-mesh strainer with the back of a spoon and discard the solids. Combine the hot juice with all but 4 teaspoons of the sugar and the blended juice in a sterilized carboy with an airlock or in a tall, nonreactive container. Allow the mixture to cool to room temperature, then stir in the yeast.

If you're not using a carboy with an airlock, cover the container without completely sealing it off (this will allow carbon dioxide to escape and keep pressure from building up). Leave the liquid out at room temperature to ferment until there's no more effervescence, about 2 weeks. Pour the liquid into 4 sterilized 750 ml bottles, putting 1 teaspoon/5 g of sugar in each, and seal the bottles.

Leave the bottles to ferment at cellar temperature for 2 days, then move the bottles to the refrigerator.

# HOW TO MAKE **PRESERVED SMELT**

Smelt are small fish that are traditionally used by the local tribes, and they make their way into many of the recipes at The Willows. We cure, smoke, and dry the small fish and use them as a seasoning in many recipes.

Smelt is widely known around the country and largely caught in freshwater with dip-nets, then battered and deep-fried. Much of our regional smelt live only in saltwater (they are still excellent fried), spawning on beaches around the sound. They have a clean ocean taste that's a bit like trout and take well to similar preparations.

Smelt present a peculiar challenge to a low-volume restaurant with a tasting-menu format. A single smelt weighs about an ounce, but since they're harvested in rather large quantities and are quite inexpensive, no one will sell you less than fifty pounds at a time. Smelt are an oily fish, and fresh specimens only stay good for two or three days, so that leaves you with a lot of fish that you need to do something with in a hurry.

We've dealt with this problem a couple of ways, but the best we've come up with is to cure and smoke them, then dry them until they are almost brittle, allowing us to turn a bunch of rapidly declining smelt into a shelf-stable product. After that, we just have to figure out what to do with a batch of 500 dried fish.

These dried smelt smell delicious, in a smoky, fishy, and slightly funky way, and have great potential. We've gone on to use them for many stocks and seasonings.

## YIELDS 20 FISH

20 fresh Nooksack River smelt (about 1 kg)
Kosher salt

With a paring knife, cut a circle around the head of each fish and slit the stomach. Grab the head at the spine, pull the spine out through the belly and discard. Rinse the bodies under cold water, completely cleaning out the cavities, and pat them dry with a paper towel. Cover the bottom of a nonreactive container with salt, place the smelt bodies on the salt, and cover them with more salt, repeating another layer, if necessary. Cover and refrigerate for 2 days. Remove the smelt and rinse them under cold running water. Pat the bodies dry and lay them in a single layer on a half-sheet pan lined with kraft paper.

Prepare a cold smoker with alderwood and cold smoke the smelt on the tray for 8 hours. Remove the tray from the smoker and set it on a counter to dry in front of a fan overnight. Flip the fish and repeat the smoking (another 8 hours) and overnight-drying process. When done, they'll be fairly rigid with just a bit of flex. Store them in an airtight container at room temperature with a layer of paper towel beneath them to absorb moisture.

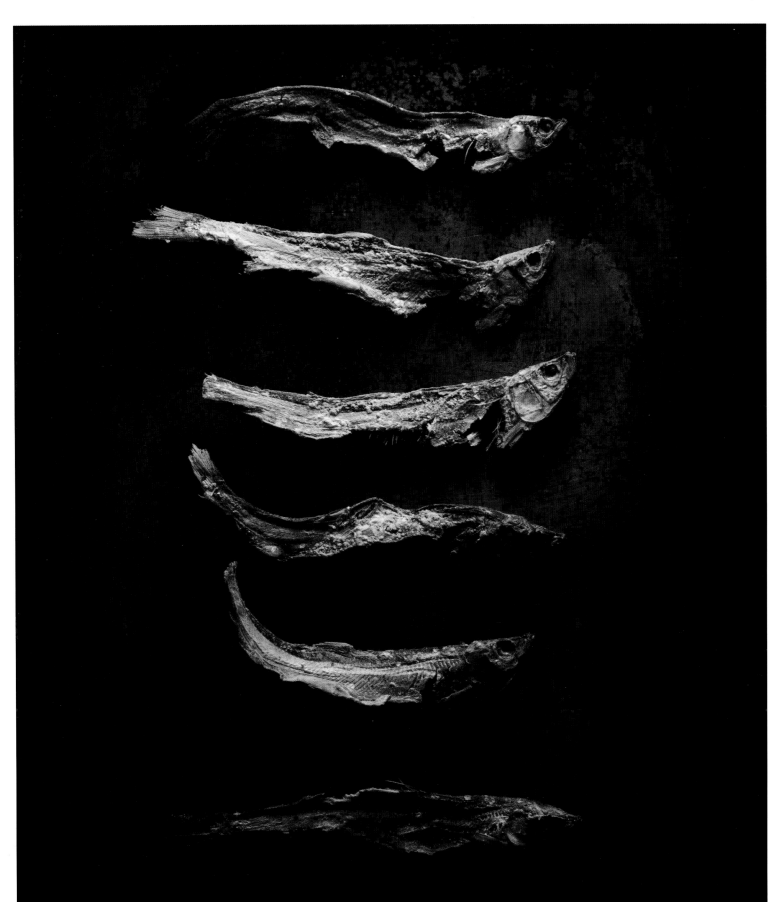

# HOW TO MAKE **PICKLED WILD THINGS**

One of the most enjoyable parts of our job is foraging for sprouts, leaves, and berries. It is a perfect change of pace and scenery after a few hours in front of the stove. In the middle of the day, I usually run out for a quick walk, either down to the beach or along one of the forest trails to collect what's needed.

We keep records of when, where, and how much of our wild foods grow here on the island. We collect as much as possible, while preserving and strengthening the wild plants, using what we can fresh and pickling what's left. Wild shoots, branches, edible mushrooms, and herbs can be quickly pickled and stored for a month simply by covering them in a hot brine and keeping them sealed in the fridge. I like to serve a mix of pickled wild shoots like these ferns along with a few other snacks and a drink on the deck right before sunset. We use fiddleheads here, but we also pickle devil's club shoots, wild onion shoots, and jelly mushrooms, keeping the amount the same.

### YIELDS 8 OUNCES/225 G FIDDLEHEAD FERNS

2 cups/450 g high-quality cider vinegar

1 cup/200 g granulated sugar

1/2 cup/25 g chopped fresh woodruff leaves and stems

1 tablespoon/5 g parsley leaves

1 fresh bay leaf

1 frond fresh dill (about 4 g)

1/4 teaspoon/1 g dill seeds

3/4 teaspoon/3 g juniper seeds

1/2 teaspoon/1.5 g whole black peppercorns

8 ounces/225 g fiddlehead ferns

In a large saucepan, bring 2 cups/475 g water, the vinegar, and the sugar to a boil and simmer until the sugar has dissolved.

Place the woodruff, parsley, bay leaf, fresh dill, dill seeds, juniper seeds, and peppercorns in a large, nonreactive container and pour the hot brine over the top. Cover the container and refrigerate it overnight.

Run the brine through a fine-mesh strainer and discard the solids.

Bring about 1 gallon/4 L of water to a boil in a stockpot. While it heats, clean the fiddleheads, trimming away any browned or woody bits of stem. Blanch the fiddleheads in the boiling water for 30 seconds. Drain them and plunge them into an ice bath until cold, then place them in the bottom of a large, plastic, nonreactive container.

Heat the brine to a simmer, pour it over the ferns, cover the container, and leave it in the refrigerator for about a week. The ferns are done when they've softened enough to uncoil without breaking but still have a bit of snap to them.

# HOW TO MAKE **FERMENTED THINGS**

Lacto-fermentation is a simple and delicious way of preserving the bounty of the harvest season. By adjusting the length and temperature of the fermentation, you can create a variety of flavors using the same ingredient. I especially like to use the flavorful brines created by this process as seasonings or sauce bases. We make large batches of fermented garlic, turnips, cabbages, and carrots mainly for their brines, which we'll use throughout the year. If any additional liquid is needed for the ferment, I generally like to use buttermilk whey instead of water, as the flavors are complementary.

YIELDS ABOUT 1 POUND/500 G GARLIC AND JUICE

1 pound/500 g green garlic, including bulb and about 3
    inches/7.5 cm of stalk
10 g salt

Roughly chop the green garlic, then place it in a medium sturdy mixing bowl and pound it with a pestle until it begins to release juice. In a separate container, mix the salt and 2 cups plus 6 tablespoons/500 g water and pour it over the garlic until all of the garlic is covered. Cover the garlic and water with parchment paper cut to fit directly on the surface to keep all solids submerged, then cover the bowl with cheesecloth. Store the mixture at room temperature for 2 to 3 weeks, or until the flavor is fully acidified, then store it in the refrigerator.

# HOW TO MAKE **CAPERS OUT OF SEEDS AND THINGS**

Chuck and Sharon at Three Pheasants Farm have an apple orchard on the island, where they grow dozens of the most flavorful varieties of apples I have ever tasted. In the spring, they take the extra step of picking half of the barely developed apples from each tree to ensure the best-possible-tasting fruit later in the fall. The small, underdeveloped apples that they thin out make perfect capers, a Pacific Northwest version of an olive, with a somewhat similar flavor and texture.

I use the same principle with green seeds or underdeveloped fruit from many wild herb and berry plants to make capers for the following season. I have not found very many things that do not cure well using this method. Here are some we've had particular success with.

### SEEDS:

Nasturtium, lovage, dill, parsley, coriander, chervil, angelica, arugula, woodruff, beet, cabbage, beach mustard, sea kale, green wild berries

### UNDERRIPE FRUIT:

Elderberry, gooseberry, currants, grapes, apples, pears

The brine is sometimes more useful than the seeds, so cover the seeds with plenty of vinegar.

YIELDS 8 OUNCES/250 G CAPERS

8 ounces/250 g small, unripe apples, no larger than ½ inch/1 cm across
8¾ ounces/250 g kosher salt
High-quality cider vinegar

Bury the whole apples in the salt in a sealed plastic container and refrigerate for a month. Rinse the apples thoroughly and soak them in 2 quarts/2 L of water for 15 minutes. Change the water and soak another 15 minutes, repeating the process until the apples have a salty but palatable flavor.

Place the apples in a plastic container with a tight-fitting lid, cover with cider vinegar, close the lid, and refrigerate for a month.

# HOW TO MAKE **FLAVORFUL HERB OILS**

These herb oils have the flavor of a fistful of just-picked leaves in every drop. We use them in some recipes instead of other fats or fresh leaves, keeping the menu light but full of flavor. It is key to blend the herbs with the oil until steam bellows out of the top of the blender and the emulsion is visibly separated.

These super-potent herb oils hold the bright flavor of fresh herbs throughout the year, essentially extending their season by months. This recipe is a real blender breaker, but it is well worth the occasional burnout and the unbelievable racket of hours of continuous high-speed blending.

YIELDS 1 QUART

1 cup/200 g grapeseed oil
1 pound plus 5 ounces/600 g herb leaves

Heat the oil to 140°F/60°C. Put the hot oil in a heavy-duty blender, add the herbs, and blend on high for 15 minutes, which will both cook the herbs and evaporate the water they contain. Crack open the blender lid slightly to let steam escape. Pour the liquid into a saucepan over ice to stop the cooking, then strain the liquid through cheesecloth (don't squeeze or the solids will be pushed out), tying the ends together and suspending the cloth over a bowl in the fridge overnight to extract as much oil as possible.

# **SEEDED RYE BREAD** (A.K.A. FIVE-DAY RYE)

**FOR DAY 1**

1³⁄₄ cups/330 g cracked rye berries

1¹⁄₄ cups/165 g raw sunflower seeds

³⁄₄ cup/115 g flax seeds

¹⁄₃ cup/35 g kosher salt

¹⁄₂ cup plus 2 tablespoons/135 g cultured buttermilk

¹⁄₄ cup/60 g 100% hydration coarse rye bread starter

**FOR DAY 5**

1 cup plus 1 tablespoon/135 g all-purpose flour

1¹⁄₂ cups/120 g coarse rye flour

2 tablespoons/17 g black malted barley powder

¹⁄₄ cup/65 g dark beer (stout or porter)

.8 ounces/23 g compressed fresh yeast

Nonstick cooking spray

1¹⁄₄ cups/200 g flax seeds

## DAY 1

Mix the cracked rye berries, sunflower seeds, flax seeds, kosher salt, buttermilk, and bread starter in a large container with 1⅓ cups/330 g water. Cover the container and store it for 4 days at room temperature, stirring daily.

## DAY 5

Pour the all-purpose flour, rye flour, and malted barley powder into the bowl of a stand mixer. Pour ½ cup/135 g of water and the beer into a glass bowl. Crush the compressed fresh yeast into small pieces, then add it to the water and beer, using a whisk to break the yeast into pieces no larger than coarse breadcrumbs. Add the yeast mixture to the flours in the mixer and mix on low with a dough hook until all of the loose powder is incorporated, about 1 minute.

Add about a quarter of the cracked rye berry mixture to the mixer and mix on low until incorporated—it should look like classic bread dough.

Add the rest of the rye berry mixture to the bowl and mix for another 5 minutes, occasionally scraping down the sides of the bowl. The dough should now be tacky and dense with grains, with just enough dough to hold it together.

Place 3 metal loaf pans (9 x 5 x 3-inch/23 x 13 x 8 cm) on a sheet pan. One loaf pan at a time, spray a heavy coating of nonstick cooking spray inside each pan, then cover first the sides, then the bottom of the pan with flax seeds. (This works best using more flax than necessary in each pan, returning the unused flax to the bowl for the next pan.)

With wet hands, portion the dough into 3 loaves weighing 1½ pounds/650 g each. Knead the dough into an oblong shape, working out any cracks or seed clusters. Press the dough into the loaf pans, working it into the corners and giving it a roughly flat top. Coat the tops of the loaves with a density of flax seeds equal to the interior of the pans.

Cover the pans with a towel and allow the dough to proof at room temperature for 4 hours, or until doubled in bulk.

Preheat the oven to 375°F/190°C. Press any air out of the risen loaves using your hands to ensure a nice, solid loaf and arrange the loaves on a half-sheet pan so air can circulate between them. Bake for 1½ hours, flipping the loaves over inside their pans after the first 45 minutes. When done, the loaf will feel lighter and the crust will be caramelized and fully set. Cool the loaves on a wire rack. They can be wrapped tightly in plastic wrap and frozen at this point.

# MUSSEL STOCK

YIELDS ABOUT 3 QUARTS/3 L

15 pounds/7 kg cleaned mussels
Reduced white wine (page 251)

Seal the mussels in a pressure cooker large enough to allow the shells to open while they cook. Cook over high heat until the cooker reaches full pressure, then maintain the high pressure and cook for 15 minutes. Give the cooker a shake, remove it from the heat, and allow it to cool before opening. Strain all of the liquid in the bottom of the pressure cooker through a Superbag. Season with reduced white wine.

# CLAM STOCK

YIELDS ABOUT 1½ QUARTS/1.5 L

¼ cup/60 g white wine
10 pounds/4.5 kg medium clams

Bring the wine to a boil in a stockpot over high heat. Add the clams and drop the heat to low. Cook the clams for 10 minutes.

Pass the stock through a fine-mesh strainer, shaking well to make sure all of the liquid comes out of the clam shells.

# SMELT STOCK

YIELDS ABOUT 2 CUPS/100 G

8 cured, dried smelt (page 236)

¼ cup/60 g white wine

8 dried shiitake mushrooms (about 12 g)

Salt

½ teaspoon packed/2.5 g dark brown sugar

Soak the smelt in a medium saucepan half-filled with cold tap water for 10 minutes. Drain and discard the water, add the white wine, dried shiitakes, and 2 cups/475 g of water to the pan and bring the liquid to a boil over medium heat. Once it boils, cover and allow the mixture to steep off the heat for 10 to 15 minutes. Taste as it steeps and adjust the seasoning with salt, if necessary, or dilute with water if the flavor seems overly smoky or salty. Remove the smelt from the pan—they can be reused for a future batch of stock, just skip the initial soaking step—and strain the liquid through a Superbag or fine-mesh strainer. Stir in the brown sugar and recheck the seasonings.

# SPINACH PURÉE

YIELDS ABOUT 1 CUP/200 G

1 pound/500 g spinach

Bring about 4 quarts/3.75 L of water to a boil in a stockpot. Add the spinach and boil for 5 minutes. Drain, then use a slotted spoon or spider to quickly transfer the spinach into an ice bath to stop the cooking. Once cool, drain, then use your hands to squeeze any excess water out of the spinach and place it in the blender. Blend on low, adding 1 or 2 tablespoons of water, if necessary, to get it to start liquefying, then blend on high until it achieves a pudding-like consistency. Store it in the refrigerator.

Parsley purée can be made in the same fashion. Just substitute parsley leaves for spinach.

# ONION STOCK

YIELDS ABOUT 1 QUART/1 L

Grapeseed oil
25 large yellow onions, peeled and halved lengthwise
1 cup/200 g chicken drippings (page 191)
1 sprig thyme
½ fresh bay leaf
1 sprig parsley

Preheat the oven to 200°F/93°C. Pour a thick layer of grapeseed oil into a pair of skillets over high heat. Working in batches, sear the flat surface of the onions until deep brown and nearly burnt.

Place the onions and chicken drippings in a stockpot and add 1 gallon/4 L of water, then cover the pot with a layer of plastic wrap, followed by a layer of aluminum foil, and finally the lid (we want to seal it tight!). Set it in the oven for 12 hours. The onions will emerge mushy and barely holding together, and the liquid will be fragrant and have a caramel color.

Strain and discard the solids. Reduce the stock, uncovered, by two thirds over medium heat. Remove from the heat, add the thyme, bay leaf, and parsley and let it sit for 10 minutes. Pass through a fine-mesh strainer and cool.

# CHARRED SCALLION PURÉE

YIELDS ABOUT 1 CUP/200 G

4 bundles scallions (about 400 g)

3 tablespoons/50 g chicken drippings (page 191)

3 tablespoons plus 1 teaspoon/50 g high-quality cider vinegar, plus more as needed

½ cup/100 g cold grapeseed oil

Salt

Prepare a grill for direct grilling. Cut the scallions in half about an inch/2.5 cm above the spot where the base turns from white to green. Grill the bulb ends over moderate heat, flipping once and stopping when they're well charred. (Reserve 1 raw bulb end for flavoring later if necessary.)

Blanch the scallion leaves in unsalted boiling water until just wilted, 20 to 30 seconds, and immediately plunge them into an ice bath. When cool, squeeze as much liquid as possible from them by pressing them against the side of a strainer with a wooden spoon.

Warm the chicken drippings in a small saucepan over low heat. Coarsely chop the blanched scallion leaves and place them into a blender with the cider vinegar. Blend for about 5 seconds, then add the charred scallion bottoms and warmed chicken drippings and continue to blend on medium until a coarse purée is formed, about 30 seconds, stopping to scrape down the inside of the blender with a spatula.

Starting with the blender on low, slowly add the grapeseed oil in a thin stream as if making mayonnaise, and gradually increase the speed until all of the oil is incorporated. Blend on high until the mixture is smooth and almost creamy, about 30 seconds. Taste the mixture, and if it's missing an identifiable raw onion flavor, add a teaspoon of sliced, raw scallion bulb to the blender and blend again until it's incorporated.

Immediately pass the purée through a fine-mesh strainer and into a metal bowl over ice. Season with salt, if necessary, and a few drops of cider vinegar.

# LIGHT VEGETABLE STOCK

YIELDS ABOUT 2 QUARTS/2 L

1 medium yellow onion

½ medium carrot, peeled

1 stalk celery

1 celeriac (about 100 g), peeled

1 green apple

1-inch/2.5 cm piece fresh horseradish root (about 35 g),
    peeled and roughly chopped

2 large parsley stems

1 fresh or 2 dried bay leaves

1 small sprig thyme

Chop the onion, carrot, celery stalk, celeriac, and green apple into a 1-inch/2.5 cm dice and place them in a stockpot with the horseradish and 2 quarts/2 L water. Bring the liquid to a simmer over medium-high heat, add the parsley stems, bay leaves, and thyme, then simmer gently until the stock takes on a golden color and delicate flavor, about 30 minutes. Strain the stock through a fine-mesh strainer.

# MUSHROOM STOCK

YIELDS ABOUT 1 CUP/235 G

1 pound/450 g button mushrooms

Grapeseed oil

4 ounces/110 g dried yellow foot chanterelles

1 sprig thyme

1 fresh bay leaf

1 sprig parsley

Salt

Cut the button mushrooms into ½-inch/1 cm slices.

Place a large Dutch oven over medium-high heat. Working in batches to prevent overcrowding, coat the bottom of the Dutch oven with grapeseed oil and sauté the button mushrooms, removing them when they're just starting to brown but are still raw inside. Off the heat, return the still-hot button mushrooms to the Dutch oven, add the chanterelles, thyme, bay leaf, and parsley, then cover and allow them to steam for at least 2 hours.

When cool enough to handle, strain out the mushroom stock, then strain the mushrooms again with a Superbag to extract any remaining liquid. Season the stock with salt.

# FRESH CHEESE

YIELDS ABOUT 1½ CUPS/300 G

1¼ cups plus 1 tablespoon/310 g raw goat's milk

¾ tablespoon/11 g very fresh heavy cream

1 teaspoon/5 g cultured buttermilk

¼ teaspoon/1 g veal rennet

Preheat the oven to 150°F/65°C.

Mix the goat's milk, cream, and buttermilk together in a metal pan small enough for the milk to be at least 1 inch/2.5 cm deep. Place the rennet in a small bowl. Pour half of the dairy mixture in with the rennet, then return it to the metal pan and give the mixture a gentle stir.

Cover the pan and place it in the oven until the cheese begins to solidify, taking on the texture of a delicate silken tofu and pulling away from the side of the pan when tipped, 7 to 10 minutes.

Reserve in a warm place until ready to use.

# REDUCED WHITE WINE

YIELDS ABOUT 1½ CUPS/375 G

1 750 ml bottle dry white wine

Reduce the wine by half in a saucepan over medium heat.

# CURED SALMON ROE

YIELDS ABOUT 2 TABLESPOONS

1 skein very fresh salmon roe (about 100 g)
Salt

Nest a 2-inch-/5 cm-deep perforated hotel pan inside a 4-inch-/10 cm-deep nonperforated hotel pan and fill it with cold seawater until it comes halfway up the side of the perforated pan. Working next to a sink, run a tap on hot and hold the skein, membrane-side up, under the hot water until the membrane constricts, 10 to 15 seconds. (If there's no constriction, the water should be hotter.) Plunge the skein into the seawater, then put the opposite side of the skein under the running hot water for 2 to 3 seconds and return it to the cold seawater.

Massage the skein with your hands to start coaxing the individual eggs to release from the membrane.

Repeat the hot/cold water process several times until all the individual eggs have been released. (You'll need to massage the smaller, individual clumps of egg toward the end.)

Scoop out the eggs, place them into a tall storage container, and cover them with fresh, cold water. Agitate the container gently, and once the eggs have sunk to the bottom, skim off any membranes that remain on the surface.

Completely drain all water from the storage container and cover the eggs with a 10 percent salt solution by weight (100 grams of salt to 1 liter of water). Keep the roe in the brine until the eggs are plump and translucent, about 15 minutes. Drain the brine, reserving a teaspoon of it, and taste an egg—you want it to have a pleasant saltiness. If it's a bit too salty, soak the eggs in cold, fresh water for a few minutes. Store the roe in a sterilized jar and pour the reserved teaspoon of brine over the top. It will keep for at least a month in the refrigerator.

# SEA SALT

YIELDS ABOUT 1 CUP

2 gallons/7.5 L seawater

Boil the seawater until it becomes sludge-like but not yet crystallized. Pour it into a half-sheet pan and set it out in the sun until dry and crystallized.

# MERINGUE

YIELDS ABOUT 1 QUART/1 L

1/3 cup plus 1 tablespoon/85 g granulated sugar

1 1/2 tablespoons/30 g corn syrup

1/4 cup/60 g fresh egg whites from Riley Starks (about 2 large eggs' worth)

Combine the sugar, corn syrup, and 2 tablespoons of water in a small saucepan and heat over high heat, without stirring, until it reaches 243°F/117°C.

In a medium metal mixing bowl, beat the egg whites with an electric mixer set at medium speed until soft peaks form. With the mixer still on medium, add the sugar mixture to the whites in a thin stream and, once incorporated, beat on high until stiff peaks form. Continue beating until the bowl is cool, then put the meringue into a piping bag.

# STOCK SYRUP

Sugar
Water

Heat equal weights sugar and water in a saucepan over medium heat until the sugar melts. Store the syrup in the refrigerator.

# DARK SYRUP

YIELDS ABOUT 2 CUPS/400 G

2 tablespoons/12 g dark malt powder
1 cup/200 g granulated sugar
¼ cup/75 g beet juice
¼ cup/55 g verjus

Sift the malt powder and sugar into a small saucepan, add ⅓ cup/65 g of water, and set over medium heat until the temperature reaches 226°F/108°C. Remove from the heat, then stir in the beet juice and verjus. Strain the syrup and store it in the refrigerator.

# ROSEMARY CANDY

YIELDS ABOUT 5 CUPS/1.3 KG

Scant ⅔ cup/200 g glucose syrup

4½ cups/1 kg grade AA isomalt

4 cups/80 g fresh rosemary leaves

Heat the glucose syrup and isomalt in a medium saucepan over medium-low heat, stirring every 2 to 3 minutes until liquid, then raise the heat to medium high and bring it to 410°F/210°C. It should have a light caramel color and take about 20 minutes.

Carefully stir in the rosemary leaves and immediately pour the hot candy onto a baking sheet with a Silpat mat and allow it to cool on a metal or stone surface. (We've learned from experience that the heat can mark wood.)

When cool, break the candy into shards no larger than 2 x 2 inches/5 x 5 cm. Place about a cup of shards into a heavy-duty blender. Pulse the blender about 4 times to start breaking up the shards. Starting on low and working up to high speed, reduce the candy to a powder, leaving only tiny bits of rosemary, no more than 10 seconds total. Continue working a cup at a time until all the rosemary candy is turned into powder.

Preheat the oven to 300°F/150°C and line a half-sheet pan with a Silpat mat. Pass about ¼ cup of the powder through a sieve, evenly coating the mat to a thickness where the Silpat has just disappeared beneath the powder.

Place the half-sheet pan in the oven until the powder has just melted—about 1 minute—then remove immediately. Allow the sheet to cool for about 20 seconds—the mixture will harden right away. Drag the tip of a spoon down one edge of the candy and gently peel the Silpat away, working to keep the sheet of candy together in large pieces. Repeat until all of the powdered candy is transformed into the finished product.

Store the pieces between sheets of parchment paper on a sheet pan and wrap the pan with plastic wrap.

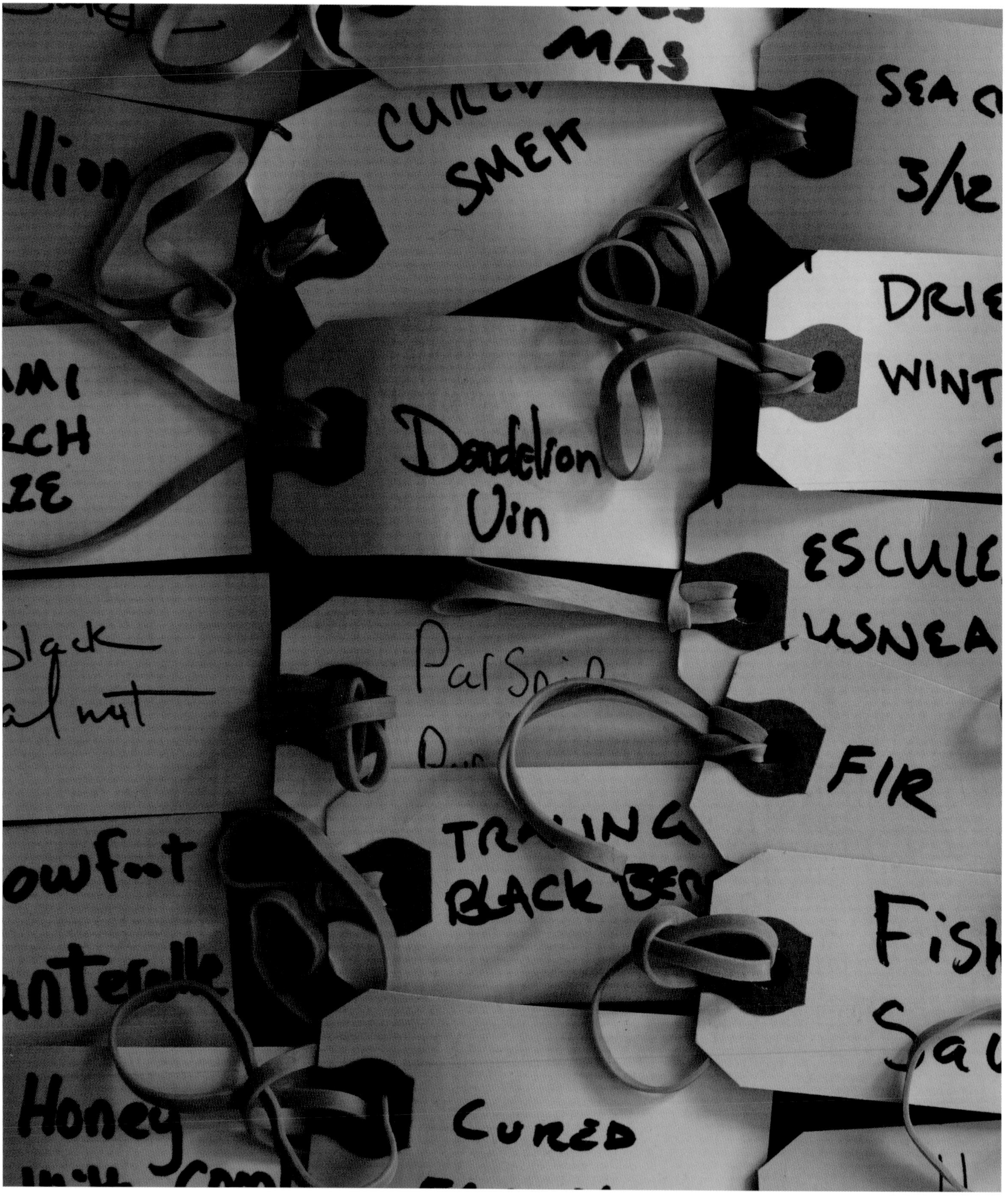

MAS
3/12
Dandelion
Vin
USNEA
FIR
Black
Fish
Honey
CURED

# ACKNOWLEDGMENTS

Thank you to the team at The Willows, who continually inspire me with their passion, hard work, and creativity; and to our amazing community of artisans, who supply the restaurant with their passions. I should also say thank you to Joe for making me write this book!

—Blaine Wetzel

Windswept thanks to the members of the Northern Rattlesnake Swim & Beach Club for your years of help and support: Elisabeth, Mom and Dad, Ben and Gina, Eli and Rosa. Thank you to charter members Lyle and Jane for dock space and support way back when this was just an idea, and to the Hortons for a seat at the table. Special gratitude to honorary club members, Tara, Lylah, the Whites and the Eaves, and a wink down the island to Moonlight Bay. Thank you to Andrew and Charity, along with Kristen and everyone at Running Press. Up in the PNW, thank you to Riley Starks, Julie and Steve, Mary, and, of course, Blaine, Nick, Cameron, Larkin, and the whole crew at The Willows.

—Joe Ray

# INDEX

Pages in *italics* refer to photos

SEA AND SMOKE